FOLLIES

Follies

An Architectural Journey

Rory Fraser

ZULEIKA

First published 2020

by Zuleika Books & Publishing

Thomas House, 84 Eccleston Square
London, SW1V 1PX

Copyright © 2020 Rory Fraser

The right of Rory Fraser to be identified
as author of this work has been asserted in
accordance with sections 77 and 78 of the
Copyright, Designs and Patents Act 1988.

All rights reserved. No part of this book may be
reprinted or reproduced or utilized in any form or by any
electronic, mechanical, or other means, now known or
hereafter invented, including photocopying and recording,
or in any information storage or retrieval system, without
permission in writing from the publishers.

British Library Cataloguing in Publication Data

A catalogue record for this book is
available from the British Library

ISBN: 978-1-9161977-8-7

Designed by Euan Monaghan

Printed in Latvia

Table of Contents

Introduction..xi

EARLY

Walsingham Priory, Norfolk.. 1
Freston Tower, Suffolk..6
Rushton Triangular Lodge, Northamptonshire.................................... 10
Swarkestone Pavilion, Derbyshire.. 16
The East Banqueting House, Chipping Campden, Gloucestershire...... 21
The Mound, New College, Oxford......................................26

CLASSICAL

Christ Church Greyfriars, The City of London, London..................... 30
The Temple of the Four Winds, Castle Howard, Yorkshire................. 35
Needle's Eye, Wentworth Woodhouse, Yorkshire...............................40
The Temple of British Worthies, Stowe, Buckinghamshire................. 44
Worcester Lodge, Badminton, Gloucestershire..................................... 49
The Palladian Bridge, Prior Park, Bath................................... 53
The Temple of Apollo, Stourhead, Wiltshire..............................56

ROMANTIC

King Alfred's Tower, Stourhead, Wiltshire........................... 61
Jack the Treacle Eater, Yeovil, Somerset................................. 63
Garrick's Temple to Shakespeare, Hampton, London.......................... 67
The Great Pagoda, Kew, London.. 72
The Temple of Venus, West Wycombe, Buckinghamshire................... 76
Clytha Castle, Monmouthshire.. 82
Broadway Tower, Worcestershire.. 86
Sezincote House, Gloucestershire... 91

MODERN

Faringdon Tower, Oxfordshire..96
The Apollo Pavilion, Peterlee, County Durham............................. 100
The Headington Shark, Oxford.. 104
The Teapot Obelisk, Deene Park, Northamptonshire......................... 108

vii

As children go, I was an odd one. You know the type: small, spatially challenged and dressed in lurid hand-me-downs. I was what kind relatives would refer to as 'a late developer'. As with most 'late developers', I sought something to distract myself from the grim business of growing up. Whilst some opted for karate, others computer games, I chose history – or rather drawing it. At first, it was everything from Aphrodite to the sinking of the *Titanic*, but as time went on, I became increasingly captivated by the places in which these events occurred – by architecture.

At secondary school, these interests were actively encouraged by my teachers. With this newfound license, and under the expert guidance of my new friend Ralph, son of a distinguished local architect, we were allowed to cycle off into the Shropshire hills and explore first-hand the history and houses of that ancient borderland – armed with the keys to many of the church roofs.

It was like this that Mr Schützer-Weissmann found us. 'Schutz', as we viii | *Follies*

later knew him, was the king of the English faculty and heir to Frank McEachran, the intellectual model for Hector from *The History Boys*. On entering our final year, Ralph and I received a mysterious invitation from Mr Schützer-Weissmann to join the 'Building Society'. This, we were told, existed to 'promote the knowledge, understanding and love of fine architecture, but its embrace is not confined to buildings or indeed to materials things'. The principal activity of the society was to meet for fortnightly papers given by members and, on field days, to visit places of architectural interest where 'modest refreshments' were usually provided. Other than this we knew nothing more, except that the pleasure of our company was 'earnestly solicited'.

A few days later, we made our way down to 'Chateau Schutz', a place that was to become our second home over the course of the following months. In Schutz's sitting room, dominated by a Bechstein grand piano, piles of sheet music and books, we were introduced to a netherworld of untapped knowledge to which we should aspire. Talks ranged from crusader tombs to the lighting of Versailles and the representation of architecture in Waugh's *Decline and Fall*. This was accompanied by the delicious claret that Schutz had collected over many summers spent perusing the vineyards of France with his wife and twelve children. Most exciting of all, however, were the jubilant emails announcing a field trip, all signed off with the same flourish: '*A Plus Tard and Plus Fours, Floreat Aedificatii*!'

Perhaps the best of these trips was to Wenlock Priory, an Anglo-Saxon monastery in Much Wenlock, founded by King Merewalh of Mercia in 680 and still lived in today. Once inside, we were given a tour by the owners through a labyrinth of candlelit rooms, ending before a roaring fire. Here, lolling on Persian rugs in a haze of wood smoke, we talked late into the night. This was the Building Society at its best: a fellowship of young men and women that, using architecture as a focal point between the aesthetic and the academic, provided a safe space in which to intellectually unfurl.

After A levels, Schutz persuaded me to apply to Oxford for English. In the months preceding my matriculation, I travelled to Kenya where I spent time with an ex-pupil of Schutz, a writer and war correspondent. On his farm, deep in the Rift Valley, we enthused about the same texts that Schutz had taught us under a blue Laikipian moon.

During my time at university, we lost Schutz to cancer. At his funeral, the aisles heaved with generations of teachers, students and Old Builders. It was a testament to his kindness, insight and wit. He was a man who not only seemed to understand life, but knew how to enjoy it and to share it with others. I was left with a powerful desire to remember Schutz by sharing with others what I was no longer able to cherish with him.

Back at Oxford, that desire was met in the unexpected form of Alexander Pope: the eighteenth-century satirist, translator, poet and garden designer, who we were covering that term. It was as though a hand had reached out from the past and taken mine. Sensing my enthusiasm, my tutor suggested that I visit the Arcadian garden Pope had helped to design at the nearby Rousham House. Here, an exquisite play of light and shade, of grotto leading to glade animated by gods seemingly petrified only moments before, I found the connection that I had been looking for. A focal point between wit, architecture, landscape and literature. A subject that spanned the same cross-cultural fault lines that Schutz had introduced us to, summarised by Horace Walpole's famous line: 'Poetry, Painting, and Gardening, or the Science of Landscape, will forever by men of taste be deemed Three Sisters.'

Hidden away in the Bodleian, a place where Pope had worked some centuries before, I developed my thesis. This was centred on the idea that reading one of Pope's pastoral poems was, through its imagery, punctuation and flow, like walking through a garden, and that walking through one of Pope's gardens was, through use of vista, planting and path, akin to reading one of his poems. When clambering about the woods of Mapledurham, a childhood haunt of Pope, I realised that the precise point of convergence between these various threads lay not in the quill, but the folly, where the world of the imagination meets with the landscape around it.

Historically, the folly is an elaborate building set in a beautiful landscape that serves no purpose other than to improve the view: architecture for the sake of architecture. In reality, there aren't many of these. As Gwyn Headley and Wim Meulenkamp, authors of the definitive book on the subject explain, a folly is ideally an:

> Ostentatious, overambitious and useless structure, preferably with a wildly improbable legend attached – but in real life it must be admitted that follies defy even such broad definitions. That's the pleasure of the things: if they could be categorised and catalogued and pinned down like specimen butterflies, we would lose that frisson of excitement and mystery when another unidentified ghostly ruin looms up out of a wet wood.

In essence, they are extremely hard to define. 'The folly', they explain, 'must lie in the eye of the beholder'. By my beholding, the folly is interesting for three reasons. First, from an aesthetic perspective, perched in the best spots of the countryside, they break architectural rules. As Headley and Meulenkamp put it:

> The best among them are pure examples of accidental architecture, hurled up with energy and a blithe disregard for correct orders. In the process they inevitably enlarged the vocabulary of building, but even

now, because of their provenance, they are treated by art historians with an amused condescension, as cul-de-sacs off the broad avenue of architecture.

Second, from a historical perspective, these small, often forgotten buildings offer us an alternative view into the periods in which they were built; a diagonal glimpse of a soft underbelly that is rarely seen, revealing the dreams of those who built them when unconstrained by the contemporary equivalent of 'building regs'. They are, in other words, the architectural embodiment of what makes people tick. In the case of Pope, for example, it was to recreate the classical world in England – one that he often retreated to in his imagination but had been unable to visit because of illness.

And third, the stories that come with them. From the smuggling den for the Prince Regent at Luttrell's Tower, to the makeshift spire erected overnight by Mad Jack Fuller to win a geographical bet. This is quite apart from the Duke of Norfolk's farmsteads praising America's fight for independence, the obelisk at Stainborough Castle, dedicated to Mary Wortley Montagu for pioneering smallpox inoculations in 1720, or the Maori House at Clandon Park, shipped over by the outgoing Governor of New Zealand, who so liked the country that he named his son Huia. These often bizarre tales, when read in parallel with the buildings' equally whacky designs, speak of an enduring national characteristic of which I was first sceptical but am now sure: an irrepressible love of individualism.

Follies are not just 'portals' into different periods, combining landscape, literature and aesthetics into brick and stone, but monuments to a remarkably liberal culture in which such architectural self-expression was not just permitted but celebrated. Most islands are defined by their monoculture. Britain draws strength from its multi-culture. Rather xii | *Follies*

than being symbols of 'little England', follies are symbols of 'bigger England', the direct result of a country formed of Celts, Romans, Angles, Saxons, Jutes, Vikings, Normans, Huguenots, wave upon wave leading down to the Schützer-Weissmanns as they left Budapest for London in the 1930s.

Within this book, through a series of sketches, both visual and verbal, I seek to record some of the best, most beautiful examples of this architectural self-expression. In so doing, I hope to provide my reader with an alternative view of this island, where the past jostles with the present at every bus stop and, if we listen carefully, asks to take us by the hand and celebrate its delights.

The week after leaving university, therefore, I packed my paints, wheeled out my car and made for the road.

To Schutz

1. Walsingham Priory
2. Freston Tower
3. Rushton Triangular Lodge
4. Swarkestone Pavilion
5. The East Banqueting House
6. The Mound
7. Christ Church Greyfriars
8. The Temple of the Four Winds
9. Needle's Eye
10. The Temple of British Worthies
11. Worcester Lodge
12. The Palladian Bridge
13. The Temple of Apollo
14. King Alfred's Tower
15. Jack the Treacle Eater
16. Garrick's Temple to Shakespeare
17. The Great Pagoda
18. The Temple of Venus
19. Clytha Castle
20. Broadway Tower
21. Sezincote House
22. Faringdon Tower
23. The Apollo Pavilion
24. The Headington Shark
25. The Teapot Obelisk

here is something quietly exotic about Norfolk, with its blue fields of lavender whose furrows rise and fall, as though ripples across a sea of lilac, more in keeping with Provence than the East Midlands. Deep within the county, tucked between Houghton St Giles and Little Snoring, lies the sleepy village of Walsingham. This is home to the remains of Walsingham Priory, one of the most beautiful monastic ruins in England and one of our earliest follies.

Put the clock back five hundred years and Walsingham was not a quaint English village but one of the three greatest pilgrimage sites in Christendom, the centre of a cosmopolitan network that extended from Canterbury to Constantinople. It was famed for a copy of the stable where Christ was born which, according to the dubious 'Pynson Ballad', was described to Lady Richeldis de Faverches by the Virgin Mary via a dream vision in 1061 – perhaps the first example of subcontracting by spiritual medium in England. Though it's hard to imagine the three wise men, perched on top of camels, wobbling down Walsingham High

2 | *Follies*

Street, the difficulty of travelling to the crusade-ravaged Holy Land meant that the village became a substitute – like Mini Venice in Las Vegas today. As such, Walsingham gained major celebrity, an ethereal name that echoed from every brothel in London to the Papal Court in Rome, rivalling Santiago de Compostela and even Jerusalem itself.

Driving through the countryside, I imagined the many pilgrims that had gone before me, bobbing their way through the landscape, clad in grey cloaks and broad hats, their staffs tapping rhythmically against the road; or at night, gathered around fires to ward off wild boar and wolves, checking their progress by the stars which, according to legend, were said to lead to Walsingham. When close, this group would have reached the Slipper Chapel, a sacred boundary that marks the start of the 'Holy Mile' to the Priory, which pilgrims typically walked barefoot.

I chose to follow in their footsteps. Hobbling along the hedgerows, I tried to imagine the sort of company that I would have had. Contrary to popular belief, most of these figures were not humourless zealots but ordinary men and women for whom it was the closest thing to a holiday or, for the younger pilgrims, a dating app that medieval society allowed.

In the 'General Prologue' to Chaucer's *Canterbury Tales*, we are given a wonderful sense of these more human figures. On approach, we might first have heard the Wife of Bath, a large widow, 'well wimpled' and slightly deaf, wittering about her various husbands, accompanied by the prim Prioress, Madame Eglantine and a Knight, haggard from his most recent crusade. Close by, no doubt, would have been the social climbing Friar, Hubert, audibly berating the Monk who openly admits to having no interest in religion at all and much prefers hunting. Straggling at the back is the motley Ploughman whose conversation – fairly dung specific – is evenly matched by the Miller, who has a fondness for breaking down doors with his head, as well as the Cook, who has an unfortunate boil which puts everyone off their food. Jangling between them all, meanwhile, is the Pardoner – by far the least popular member of the group – loaded with all manner of pig bones and rags, which he attempts to pass off as relics.

I continued walking until the road funneled between two high flint walls, before spilling out into the village square. This must have presented an awesome site, its cobbles clattering with wealthy merchants up from London, cross-eyed clerics from monasteries in darkest fen, mysterious figures, smelling of cinnamon, fresh from the great ports at Antwerp, Le Havre, Cadiz or, better still, the crimson flash of a cardinal and glittering train of a king. For Walsingham was visited by every monarch from Henry III to Henry VIII. Given the efficiency with which the latter managed to destroy most monastic buildings in the Reformation, I was curious as to what remained.

After winding along a path overhung with yew I came out onto a great pool of lawn. In the centre of this is not the usual tattered remains of a cloister, or gaunt skeleton of a nave, but instead what looks like a doorway fit for giants: a magnificent arch soaring high above the tree line, its sheer size rendering everything around it, including the handsome Palladian house that has grown from its ruins, utterly insignificant. For a moment, I was silenced. Whilst most medieval enthusiasts harp on about the majesty of Fountains Abbey or scale of Rievaulx – also incorporated into landscape gardens – there is something deeply magnetising about this ruin. Its lack of context and warm, pinkish glow make it all the more mysterious.

On closer inspection, it transpires that this is the remains of the East Window of the Priory which, judging by the size of the arch, must have been substantial. Though hardly any of the Priory remains, the detailing around the arch more than suffices: a patchwork of cusped windows and quatrefoils traced in flint, out of which jut stone niches from which an army of saints once peered. Around

this are scattered a number of tiny doors and arrow-slit windows, hinting at the hidden corridors within – as though the statues are merely hiding. All of this feeds, however, into the remains of the East Window which hangs, floating in the air, like the strands of a once intricate cobweb.

It is this window that captivates. Like a great portal, it draws the eye in, murmuring of the world that once existed behind its polychromatic scheme: of black canons who, with their white habits and cloaks, led the 'press of peares' and palmers that thronged through the Priory's mighty doors, chanting the 'sweetest himnes' that rose above the veil of incense and up into its gleaming towers whose 'golden, glittering tops / Pearsed once to the sky'. All of this to see the shrine of Our Lady, an inner sanctum described by a young Erasmus, visiting from Cambridge, as a tiny wooden chapel, dark but for the tapers which glowed inside, revealing a 'sete mete for sayntes ... wt gold, syluer, and precious stones' leading to a relic: the 'heuenly mylke of Our Lady ... closyd in crystalle ... mylkyd more than a thowsand and fyue hundrithe yere agone'.

I stirred from my dream vision not at the nudge of a canon but the sound of an oncoming fleet of vicars. So engrossed had I been in the past that I had forgotten that Walsingham is still a major draw for pilgrims today, welcoming over 300,000 visitors a year from across the globe. Whilst I had initially been suspicious of the concept of 'England's Nazareth', now I was not so sure. As I wandered back through the garden, I began to feel a sense of peace. It was as though, once destroyed, the sanctity of the shrine had bled out into the landscape, marking it forever.

As I made for the exit, I was stopped by a gaggle of Italian pilgrims who, fizzing with excitement, shook my hand vigorously and invited me to join them in prayer. Standing in a circle, we closed our eyes

6 | *Follies*

and clasped hands. After saying a Hail Mary and blessing each of the company, they asked the Virgin to watch over me, my book and journey, granting me safe passage. Not only was I incredibly touched but inspired. For in many ways, I was indeed at the beginning of a pilgrimage, one where I hoped to commune, not with a living God, but a living past; as Chaucer wrote: '[to] seek out foreign strands / To far-off shrines, renowned in sundry lands'.

As a region, when perhaps your main claim to fame is being flat, you're not doing very well. Despite this, I've always had a soft spot for the Fens: an ancient realm of monasteries and mists, of Saxon rebel Hereward the Wake, King John's lost crown lurking deep beneath the mud flats, and Ely Cathedral, home to St Etheldreda's shrine, soaring high above them. There is something otherworldly about them. Personally, I think it's the light. At first, you might notice it in the dappled corner of a room, or flecks dancing under a bridge, but the further you drive, the more you notice, until suddenly this light is everywhere, enveloping everything with a crystalline clarity that lifts you clean out of yourself and up into a sparkling new world of sun, sea and sky. It's no wonder that local boy, the landscape painter John Constable, wrote that: 'the sky is the source of light in nature and it governs everything'. Through it, you notice all: every hair of corn, every flake of frost. In winter, it lends the horizon a vastness, whilst in summer, an intimacy where the patchwork of meadow, river and reed is transformed into a theatre set where the actors aren't so much people but flora.

Deep within Constable country lies Freston, an ancient name meaning the place or farm of the Frisians – who formed part of the Saxon melting pot. A flash of red alerted me that I was close. A handbrake turn later and I was rumbling my way along a dirt track through what looks like a medieval hunting forest bristling with oak, sweet chestnut, cedar and beech. I turned a corner, and there it was — Freston Tower, the first official folly in England, bathing in the midday sun. It looks out across a magnificent view that sweeps down to the great Orwell Estuary, over fields of sea kale and samphire, and out to sea.

Other than its date, which has been traced to 1578, the tower remains shrouded in mystery. At first glance, it's as though a giant has lopped off a corner of Hampton Court and plonked it down in the middle of nowhere. I half expected to see Henry VIII swaggering around the corner or Anne of Cleves scampering into the undergrowth. Spotting neither, I went for a closer look.

Built at the height of Elizabethan England, the brickwork is beautifully mottled. Smoked browns and dusty reds form a narrow base, in turn fretted with diamonds in charcoal blue that rise up the side, culminating in four fantastic finials. The more I looked at it, the more confused I became. Whilst the local legends are various, some suggesting the tower was used as a lookout post for pirates, others a way of keeping tabs on the many ships carrying wine, lace and corn to the bustling port at Ipswich, the most popular suggests that it was built for the education of a fourteenth-century Rapunzel named Ellen de Freston. According to the legend, each floor served a different lesson: charity, tapestry, music, literature and astrology – the early modern equivalent of home economics – with the latter providing ample opportunity for her to fall into the arms of her lascivious tutor, William Latimer. I love the images conjured up by this: casket-like rooms strewn with looms, lyres and star charts, neglected by a whimsical girl who would rather spend hours gazing out of the window, dreaming of Spanish galleons and the Aztecs.

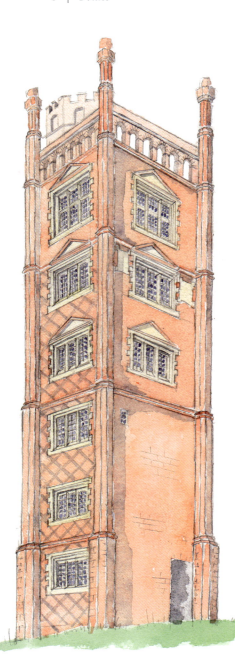

Given the date, this is – alas – total rubbish, made up by the enterprising, and presumably rather bored, Rev. R. Cobbold in the nineteenth century, and subsequently slammed by the party-pooping, and no doubt equally bored, Rev. C.R. Durrant. However, this didn't stop it from appearing as fact in a book on East Anglian curiosities until 1992. Squabbling vicars aside, the truth perhaps lies in the building's classical detailing above the upper widows. Just as the architecture of the period was in a molten stage between the medieval and classical, so too was society between old money and new.

Cue Thomas Gooding, the archetypal socially aspiring merchant. In a pattern we shall see time and again, Gooding acquired Freston Manor, a beautiful place with dovecotes and flowerlands, an orchard of quince and pears, and roses growing in the formal gardens, in order to cement his position. Keen to broadcast this to the world, imagine Gooding's joy when he heard news of a royal progress, that the Rainbow Queen herself, Gloriana Elizabeth I would be sailing right past his patch in August of 1579. What better way to attract her languid eye than to build a massive orange tower on the starboard side – complete with a portly merchant waving frantically from the top of it.

In spite of this, there is something beautiful, even alluring about Freston. Like the landscape around it, it occupies a netherworld, standing on the cusp between land and sea, a 'face that launch'd a thousand ships' and welcomed them back again, for over four hundred years. I can't help but be reminded of the monarch for whom it was built. She too occupied a netherworld, caught between a medieval past and modern future, between the ancient hunting forests of her father and the New World beyond the seas.

Whilst the tall, slender tower, red-headed and finely decked, may never have been home to the little girl in the legend, gazing out of one of its many windows, dreaming of pirates and strange new lands, it can perhaps be seen to represent another, rather more consequential woman, for whom these things were more than real.

Whilst Freston Tower could be seen to symbolise Elizabeth's 'Golden Age', my next destination, Rushton Triangular Lodge, designed on the wall of a prison cell, represents the threat that endangered it.

Nestled deep within Northamptonshire, a landlocked county in the heart of England, Rushton couldn't be more different to Freston. Here the horizon is dominated not by water but by wood: the great Rockingham Forest, William the Conqueror's hunting park. It was towards this brooding sea of oak that I now drove. Soon enough, the trees engulfed me, and I was winding through the number of villages that scatter the forest, as though sunken in the deeps, each built in the same distinctive local ironstone, a reddish, bloody brown, often pocked and peppered with lichen, that lends the buildings an earthy texture.

There is something conspiratorial about this hushed corner of the world. Wandering through the forest, you can half mistake a gust of wind for the rustle of a poacher, or the distant bray of hounds complete with snatches of court French and the mournful roar of a stag. In 1460, the same roar could be heard not far away at the Battle of Northampton, when the county became the epicentre of the War of the Roses, perhaps earning its title 'The Rose of the Shires'.

Marching under the crimson banner of the Lancastrians was Sir Thomas Tresham, son of William Tresham, veteran of Agincourt, friend of Henry V, mentor to Henry VI, Speaker of the House, Sheriff and Squire of Rushton. A century later, the family was headed by Sir William's great grandson, Thomas Tresham, who was knighted by Elizabeth in 1575 and poised for a glittering career in the newly Protestant England. In all regards, Sir Thomas was everything to which the Goodings of this world aspire. Clad in a glistening suit of armour, fretted with gold and lace, a magnificent coat of arms with phoenix and fleur de lys emblazoned to the right of his neatly clipped moustache, Tresham's portrait exudes the confidence of a renaissance man. After studying at Oxford and the Inns of Court, Tresham returned to his estates where he not only entertained on a prodigious scale but acquired the largest library of architectural books in the country. This included works ranging from Vitruvius to Alberti, Serlio, Palladio and Philibert d'Orme, as well as works of mathematics, religion and theology – all in a host of different languages.

In his private rooms at the end of the long gallery, Tresham would pour over these books, scribbling all manner of notes in the same extravagant hand. Among these were the numbers '55'. Whilst this may not seem significant, these numbers, code for 'Jesus Maria', were treason. This, however, was the least of Tresham's concerns. For beneath the many mullioned gables of Rushton Hall, in the bowels of the house, Tresham was hiding Edmund Campion, a Jesuit missionary and priest sent from the continent to fortify the faith of England's Catholics. In 1581, Tresham was found out, arrested and tried before Star Chamber. Despite begging the judges to believe that it was possible to be both Catholic and to have a 'true English heart', he was sentenced for fifteen years, whilst Campion was disembowelled.

Once imprisoned, Tresham wasted no time. Those who visited his cell found its walls covered with strange dates, numbers, scribbles and scrawls, a mongrel scheme that more resembled an equation than a design. To the naked eye, he seemed to have gone insane, finally succumbing perhaps to the scrutiny born of the successive plots that raged across the country, each foiled by the Queen's spymaster, the unrelenting Lord Walsingham. However, Tresham's copy of Euclid's *Elements of Geometrie*, where he had translated quotations of Seneca's *Epistulae Morales* from Latin into Spanish, proves that there was method to his madness:

> *Los males, Los dolores, la pobreza, La necessidad, Las afrentas, Las carceles, y destierros quando llegan al ho[m]bre sabio pierden su furia, y se amansa todo ... el geometria me enseña medir un fosso, enséñeme ponne medida a mis desseos* [Wrongs, pain, poverty, necessity, injustice, imprisonment: these should be feared everywhere, but when they come upon the wise man, they are tamed ... Geometry teaches me how to measure a ditch, it teaches me to put a measure on my desires.]

12 | *Follies*

In other words, the patterns on the wall of his cell were a blueprint, born of morality, exercised through geometry, by which Tresham tamed his frustrations and maintained composure in captivity. On his release in 1593, he wasted no time in making this blueprint a reality.

After racing along a low, seemingly interminable estate wall, my car flashed past the folly at 60 mph. I entered its walled enclosure with a degree of trepidation. Rushton is arguably the most famous pre-classical folly in England. What if it is underwhelming? To quote one indignant review on TripAdvisor: 'built by some bloke called Tresham … I can smell something porky. There is nothing Christian about this building. I don't know which is worse: The people who make this stuff up, or the people that believe it'.

Fortunately, I'm firmly in the gullible camp. Standing in the middle of the lawn, surrounded by yew, was perhaps the most extraordinary building I have ever seen, the sort of place you might bury a 'horcrux' or find the Holy Grail. This is not least because of its triangular form which, no matter how long you gaze, the eye cannot fully comprehend. At a glance, it looks like a casket, each of its three façades inlaid with red and white limestone. In this are set a series of windows, each more amazing than the last: clovers at the base, rising to diamonds fringed with blue glass spheres, giving way to trefoils, interlaced with triangles, each framed by a cluster of crests. Crowning this is an entablature, around which runs a jumble of letters dotted with angels. These are rendered tame only by the gables above which, adorned with wild boar, sundials and serpents, rise, licking with flame, into an array of obelisks.

The more I walked around the building, the more self-conscious I became, as though I was not looking at it but it at me – as though, if I turn my head, the carved falcons will fly away, the dragons rampant topple over and its numerous eyes blink. The building was whispering in a foreign tongue that I half remembered, but not from where. It was like

14 | *Follies*

listening to a voice crackle across the radio, fragments of speech, calling, before submerging once more into silence. It was profoundly unnerving.

In part, this can be explained by the fact that, since the lodge's construction, much of its symbolism has fallen out of common reference, hence my dim, but incomplete, understanding. The building is an essay on the number three chosen, on the face of it, as a pun on 'tres' – Tresham's nickname from his wife. But more sincerely, it is an architectural expression of the Trinity. In order to express this elusive concept – especially the Trinity – Tresham turned to mathematics in much the same way that the Ottomans did geometry to convey the mystery of Allah. It is partly for this reason that the lodge has a foreign, almost oriental feel, more akin to a mosque than a church, the dappled light from its honeycomb windows alluding to the intricate screens and lattices of the East.

Instead of minarets and domes, this geometry is reflected in the length of the walls, each thirty-three feet long, the age at which Christ died. In the middle of the building, over the door, is carved '5555', not only referring to 'Jesus Maria Salus Mundi' but, if 1593, the date of Tresham's release from prison is subtracted, it leaves 3962, the supposed date of creation. Around the entablature, meanwhile, the thirty-three letters on each face read: *'quis separabit nos a charitate Christi'* ('who shall separate us from the love of Christ', Romans 8:35), *'aperiatur terra et germinet salvatorem'* ('let the earth open and bring forth a saviour', Isiah 45:8) and *'consideravi opera tua domine et expavi'* ('I have considered thy works, Lord, and have been afraid', Habakkuk 3:2), whilst the gutter-wielding angels, as though celestial trumpeters, proclaim SSSDDSQEEQEEQVE, anagram for the 'Hymn of Praise', usually sung just before communion. The result of this cocktail of heraldry, parable and myth – some of which is yet to be deciphered – is a building that not only celebrates the intangibility of the Trinity, as well as the family of the architect that designed it, but the Mass itself. Every Mass, however, needs a congregation, and for the building to have its full effect, to '*mentes tuorum visita*' ('visit the minds of thy people') and transubstantiate into a petrified version of the ritual it so longs to restore, it needs a mind to interpret it.

On reflection, I was not going mad. The Lodge is still working its magic and the voice I heard was Tresham's issuing a form of SOS across the centuries, one that not only asserts his much harassed family and faith but, crucially, attempts to catechise others into it. A similar metaphysical exercise is seen in George Herbert's poem 'The Temple' where, through constructing a church in verse, the poet attempts to build one in the minds of his readers:

Ryme thee to good, and make a bait of pleasure.
A verse may finde him, who a sermon flies,
And turn delight into a sacrifice.

It is perhaps for this reason that Pevsner, the celebrated architectural historian wrote: 'as a testament of faith this building must be viewed with respect'.

As I turned to leave the building, faith and sacrifice played on my mind. Other than to house his rabbit keeper, it is unknown exactly what Tresham used the lodge for in his lifetime. Some believe it to have been the site of illicit Masses, accessed by a secret passage from the house. Others, a place where Tresham entertained. Personally, I like to think that he used it as a place for meditation, a private space where he could pray for his old friend Campion and the countless others of an increasingly persecuted minority who died in the name of '*recusar*e', or refusal to submit to the Reformation – 'the English Inquisition'.

Among these was Tresham's son, Francis, who, disillusioned and angry at his father's humiliation, became embroiled in the Gunpowder

16 | *Follies*

Plot. After the infamous night on 5 November 1605, Francis was caught, died in custody and decapitated, his rotting head displayed over Northampton city gates which, for generations, his family had served as Sheriff. In this sense, the Lodge today is as much a stone mass as it is a memorial for a lost generation of Catholics, illustrated by the empty crests left by Tresham for future marriages, never to be filled, faceless and forgotten, now little more than a rural bus stop.

On a Sunday afternoon in 1968, a year after the Summer of Love, a Daimler crunches its way down the drive of a farmhouse in rural Derbyshire. Coming to a halt, the driver's pale hand, cradling a cigarette, winds down the window that looks out onto a beautiful Jacobethan ruin, Swarkestone Pavilion, abandoned in a field. His lip curls. Not only has he just won the race from London – the other Daimler coming in now – but the site is perfect. Mick Jagger nods, and out step the Rolling Stones.

Apart from the local town, Ashby-de-la-Zouch, which sounds more like a hapless cavalier than a Midlands manufacturing hub, what possible connection could there be between this curious building and the most famous rock band in the world? Many asked the same question as they watched the band lug a grand piano across the field before painting it white and starting a game of cricket. The answer: whimsy. For Swarkestone served as the perfect set for the Stones' new album *The Beggar's Banquet* – the interiors having been shot in London the day before, complete with several barnyard animals and some very good claret. The result is one of the most iconic photoshoots in music history.

Looking over the photographs today, we see the band dressed in a combination of harlequin hose, jerkins, top hats and tails – as though wandering minstrels meet the Artful Dodger at a *commedia dell'arte* party in Soho. They drape themselves precariously across the pavilion's skeletal façade and lounge in the long grass before it, smoke bombs streaming through the roof, as though smashed up during the night. The product is not only one of the best portraits of the band ever taken, showing them 'at their most beautifully dangerous', but also of the period, reflecting the national shift in mood towards what *Time* magazine dubbed the 'subversive roisterer'.

When the Pavilion was built, the same shift was palpable. Whilst the Tresham families fell, the merchant Goodings had been busy, resulting in a lavish period of late Elizabethan excess. Much of this is illustrated in architecture through the vast 'prodigy houses' erected across the country, where the English castle was combined with the palazzi to form houses such as Burghley to Wollaton, Hatfield and Hardwick; great glasshouses crowned with a carnival of pepper pots, finials and chimneys that are more in keeping with the Loire Chateaux of Chambord and Chenonceau than the English counties. Many of these houses were designed by the Smythson family, and Swarkestone Pavilion, built for a wealthy lawyer, was no exception.

Having been restored by the Landmark Trust, Swarkestone, in spite of its miniature scale, projects all the gravitas of its grander cousins – albeit, being only one room thick, with a subversive twist. Viewing it head-on, the effect is no less impressive: a pair of Tuscan columns rise to three ogee arches and an entablature on which sit three mullioned windows capped with crenellations. This central section is then framed by two crisp turrets, immaculately proportioned, topped with an elegant cornice, leaded cupolas and gleaming ball finials. The overall composition, executed in a buff-coloured stone tinged with grey, is exquisite. It enjoys the perfect play of massing, projection, recession and silhouette, resulting in a building that is stately but with an unmistakable air of romance.

Given that the building was designed to celebrate a marriage, with records of extra 'gloves, gauntlets and liveries' being ordered for it, this is hardly surprising. Beyond this, its purpose, along with the walled enclosure in front of it – known as the Cuttle – remains a mystery. Over the course of its life, the pavilion has been known as a grandstand, summerhouse or bullring, the latter hinting at bear baiting or even jousting competitions that became fashionable in the neo-chivalric court

presided over by Henrietta Maria, wife of Charles I. The Landmark Trust's favoured line, however, is that the enclosure was used for games of bowls, a pastime so popular in Tudor England that it began to threaten national security – distracting the nation from their archery practice. Whilst I have no doubt that games of bowls did take place, equally likely was the performance of masques – lavish, highly allegorical mini-plays, now 'de rigueur' at court. Though these were mainly performed in London under the voluptuous Rubens ceiling at the Banqueting House, complete with fairy-tale mechanical scenery by Inigo Jones, they were often put on at the great houses further afield as summer entertainments. Swarkestone would have served as the perfect backdrop.

I imagined the inhabitants of the house tumbling out of the pavilion into the Cuttle after a sumptuous banquet: quince cast every colour from rosy pink to ruby and gold, parmesan, apricot paste and biscotti, dyed with sandalwood, to be dipped in all manner of sweet wines, syrups and creams in the upper room, whose pearly walls were dressed with alabaster. Sprawled beneath the stars, wrapped in velvet and silk, they would have seen the pavilion's windows glittering against the night sky before the sound of mandolins announcing the first act. This would have featured gorgeous costumes, spangled with braid, flashing as the dancers wove elaborate shapes, drawing the viewer, as Milton put it in his masque *Comus*, across 'the starry threshold of Jove's Court' and into a world where 'immortal shapes / Of bright aerial spirits live insphered … above this spot / Which men call Earth'. Suspended, the audience would have seen the usual fight between good and evil, often enacted by members of the party themselves, with wild animals and children zip-wiring across the scene.

In the case of *Comus*, evil is illustrated through a thinly veiled parody of court where 'orient liquor in a crystal glass' designed to 'bathe the drooping spirits in delight / Beyond the bliss of dreams' alters the

20 | *Follies*

'human count'nance, / The express resemblance of the Gods … to roll with pleasure in a sensual sty', filling the air with 'barbarous dissonance'.

In 1968, as the Stones shrieked and howled their way around the pavilion, fresh from recording their new cover 'Sympathy for the Devil', one gets a strange sense of déjà vu. The song's chilling lines: 'I killed the Tsar and his ministers / Anastasia screamed in vain' recall how, on a bitter morning in January, seventeen years after the pavilion was built, Charles I, defeated in the civil war, passed under the same Rubens ceiling in the Banqueting House to meet his executioner. Indeed just as Swarkestone represents the theatricality and decadence of the Jacobethan era, its ruin represents the immense change on the horizon and England's coming of age: a paradox that the Stones never symbolised more than in this moment. A year later, having just reached their musical maturity, Brian Jones, one of their number, was found dead.

The spirit of Swarkestone, however, lives on. Hang around on a summer's evening and, if the moon is in the right position, and enough wine has flowed, you may well mistake even the doughtiest Landmark Trust visitor for a nymph darting naked around the enclosure – a challenge known as the 'Cuttle Shuttle', whose lap times can be found in the pavilion's logbook.

My next destination took me from the gaunt hills of Derbyshire to the rolling Cotswolds in what is perhaps England's most picturesque county, and one that we shall return to frequently: Gloucestershire.

On 9 May 1643, just over ten years after Swarkestone Pavilion was built, however, the sight would have been less pleasant: a tattered line of Royalist troops, part of Prince Rupert's increasingly weary army, squelching their way up Broadway Hill, their sodden muskets and pikes gleaming red against the light of a vast country house, Campden House, burning in the vale below. Whilst these men would have been no strangers to destruction, on this occasion, they may have been shocked. For not only was Campden House the home of the late Sir Baptist Hicks, the second-richest man in England and friend of the King himself, but one of the greatest houses of the age, completed only thirty years before. As one soldier put it: 'The howse (which was so faire) burnt'. As the soldiers watched the flames lick around the columns that adorned its bold façade, rising from Doric to Ionic and Corinthian, bursting out of the lantern above, they must have known that they were not just retreating but marching away from the world as they knew it.

Today, however, the road to Chipping Campden is as pleasant as ever. Cheered by the names of local towns: Moreton-in-Marsh, Honeybourne, Adlestrop and Kingham, you pass Izod's Post, a remarkably inaccurate signpost dating from 1669, before flying down a suspiciously Roman-looking road, flanked by rolling wold, and delving down into the town itself. From here, I offer a trigger warning that the following description will be devastatingly twee – Ladies in Lavender, dusted in crumpet crumbs, bellowing Jerusalem; or as A.A. Gill put it: 'snorting a line of the most pernicious and debilitating Little English drug, nostalgia. The warm, crumbly, honey-coloured, collective yesterday … where we achieved peak Blighty.' For this, I am unapologetic, for in Chipping Campden, the 'jewel in the crown of the Cotswolds', that yesterday never ended.

On arrival, you could be forgiven for thinking you had wandered into Tolkien's Shire. Thatched cottages, smothered in wisteria, line the road which opens out into a golden core seemingly carved from honeycomb. A jumble of bowed mullions and jutting gables adorned with sundials and signposts boast the town's array of shops: Draycott Books and Drinkwater's Veg, Cuts of Campden, Fillet and Bone and the Bantam Tea Rooms. All this overlooked by a magnificent church whose lime avenue is said to signify each of the apostles, complete with a priest who used to prioritise cricket over confession and end every sermon with a nod to William the Conqueror.

If this isn't enough, the town still preserves a number of ancient traditions. In the winter, allegorical mumming plays, performed by the same families since the war. In the summer, the Scuttlebrook Wake, where a local girl is crowned queen in a carriage pulled by the town's Morris men who perform a signature dance – complete with rosettes and a pig's bladder. Whilst most famous of all is the Dover's Games, the oldest Olympics in Britain. This features all manner of contests from spurning the barre to horse racing, hare coursing, and shin-kicking, ending in a torchlit procession and an almighty piss-up.

However, the beauty of the town must not be confused with anachronism, for its success lies in its remarkable adaptability over the ages. According to the Chipping Campden Historical Society, it was first colonised by the Hwicce or Dobunni tribes because of its fertility. Then by the Romans, who built Buckle Street and a number of vineyards in an optimistic attempt to remind themselves of sunnier climes. After the Romans, this plum spot fell into the hands of the Saxon Kings, namely the ill-fated Harold of Hastings fame. From 1066, it was transferred to the Norman favourite Hugh d'Avranches, known as 'the Wolf', for his personal use, before receiving a much-coveted Royal Charter in 1185. After this Chipping Campden boomed, becoming epicentre to the medieval wool trade which accounted for 50% of the national economy. Whilst more recently, it became a centre for William Morris's Arts and Crafts movement, a home to the author Graham Greene and, nowadays, the antidote to Canary Wharf for London bankers – illustrated by the most recent addition to the High Street: the Doggylicious Day Spa.

By far the most exciting moment in the town's history was its adoption by Sir Baptist Hicks – another 'Gooding', or the seventeenth-century Jeff Bezos – worth a whopping £9.2 billion in today's money and thus one of the 250 richest Britons since 1066. A cloth merchant from Cheapside, Hicks made his fortune by lending money to the perennially broke aristocracy – especially the King who, in a time of great show, needed it to buy Hicks' velvets, satins and silks for everything from coronation robes to costumes for masques. Even today, the town is still flush with his wealth, illustrated most obviously through the market hall, with a cobbled arcade, blind gables and obelisks. This stands proudly in the centre of the High Street and is so beautiful that the Americans even tried to buy it – before the Campden Trust declared Martial Law.

Better even than the market hall was Sir Baptist's country seat, Campden House. This was built in the latest style at a time when English architecture was at its most exuberant, enjoying a final Wild West before classicism's exacting specifications became entrenched. Passing between the fabulous finials and ogive pavilions that flank the main gateway, I expected a truly great house.

Instead, I met nothing: a void of green and the sound of sheep nibbling at the turf. So enthralled had I been by its surroundings that I had forgotten that the house had been frontier between the Royalist Oxford and Parliamentarian Warwick. As such it was scene to frequent skirmishes, where sleeping men were regularly 'suppriz'd … in their beds', and was eventually destroyed in the Civil War – burnt by a retreating Royalist garrison who deemed it too sensitive to leave unmanned.

All that now remains is a small, suspiciously elaborate building in the far corner of the field, known as the East Banqueting House. At first glance, with its reddish, buttery texture, it looks like frosted gingerbread – appropriate, perhaps, as this is one of the many delicious things that would have been eaten inside it. The façade facing the village features an arcade, now glazed, rising to a parapet that blooms into

diamonds, obelisks and fleur de lys, from which twirl four barley-sugar chimneys seemingly carved from marzipan, whilst the façade facing away from the village reveals a secret storey burrowed into the bank below, providing sweeping views over the landscape. The result is dazzling: an architectural bravura, half Flemish, half Baroque, enjoying a final jamboree in the Jacobethan twilight.

One can only imagine the house onto which it was designed to look. As one contemporary wrote: 'an Edifice in the boldest Style of that Day'. In the centre, a portico 'with a series of Columns of the 5 Orders ... and an open Corridore'. This rose from 'Frizes and Entablatures most profusely sculptured' to a 'Parapet with finished pediments of a capricious taste' and chimneys of 'twisted Pillars with Corinthian Capitals' crowned with a dome: 'regularly illuminated for Direction of Travellers during the Night'. From this, a 'grand Terras' formed the cusp between the house and garden, its paths radiating star-like across the parterres over which many a firework would have burst.

I was brought back to earth by the sound of some Landmark Trust visitors trundling their suitcases over the fossilised garden in a wheelbarrow. Fleeing the scene, I wandered up to Hicks' tomb in the church: a magnificent marble affair of almost papal proportions, outmatched only by the effigy of Hicks and his wife within who, swaddled in stone, lie open eyed, gazing up at their motto: '*Non Dum Metam*' ('Not Yet My Goal').

In truth, I couldn't help but see a bitter irony in Campden. For the very cause of the house's construction was also the cause of its destruction. In financially propping up the Stuart regime for so long, and making a fortune in the process, Hicks merely deepened the ensuing economic crisis that led to the Civil War. As Sir Francis Bacon, king of the London literati and friend of Hicks, once wrote: money lenders are 'the canker and ruin of many men's estates, which in the process of time breeds public poverty' – a poverty that eventually claimed Hicks' own estate.

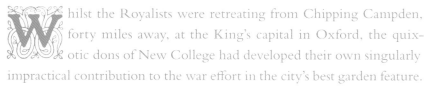

Whilst the Royalists were retreating from Chipping Campden, forty miles away, at the King's capital in Oxford, the quixotic dons of New College had developed their own singularly impractical contribution to the war effort in the city's best garden feature.

Today, the same practicality still evades Oxford. Given the byzantine complexity of its one-way system, and students' notoriously cavalier attitude to cycling, I decided to park-and-ride into the centre. Hopping off the bus outside University College, I skirted past Queen's Lane Coffee House, purportedly the oldest in Europe, before diving down Queen's Lane itself. This is one of my favourite parts of the city: at once both central and removed, as though the main corridor of some enormous ship, hinting at its many delights. First, you see the dark sash windows of Queens, still curtained. Then the crenellated gardens of New College, with purple bloom spilling over the walls. After this, the way narrows into two façades: one smooth and classical, the other rough and blackened with soot, punctuated by arrow slits that recall the clattering hooves and armour of the ghosts reported here in 1968. Above this runs a series of gargoyles, each more contorted than the last – like students mid essay-crisis – before finally ending in a shimmering vision of cupola, finial and spire; a view that whispers of the illuminated tomes, and the many minds that have read them, beyond.

A bike cavorted past me, balancing a cello across a series of books, and I leapt out of the way. Passing under Little Bridge, the forerunner to the Bridge of Sighs, I made for New College. After entering through a tiny wooden door, nothing can prepare you for the grandeur of its Front Quadrangle: the perpendicular hall and chapel soaring high above with the sound of sixteen choristers, ruffed and robed in crimson, emanating from its recesses. It is a living testament not only to the resolve of its founder, William of Wykeham, the once working-class boy turned Bishop of Winchester and High Chancellor, but the majesty of a medieval endowment, best summarised by Wykeham's uncompromising, but egalitarian motto: 'Manners Mayketh Man'. Here, under the care of his jewel-encrusted crozier, mitre and ring, Wykeham hoped to shield his students from the 'pestilence, wars and other miseries of the world', training them to become 'men of great learning, fruitful to the Church of God to the King and Realm'.

Whether this is what the dons of New College had in mind when they sanctioned the Mound remains dubious. It does not, however, diminish its effect.

I emerged into Garden Quad, a palatial edifice that unfurls into the garden. At the centre of this, framed by a golden gate, is the Mound: a pyramid of green, thirty feet high, sixty wide, with a flight of stairs leading up the middle and into the trees.

Until recently, remarkably little was known about the Mound. Some thought it was a relic of early modern gardens, like the one found at the Villa Medici in Rome, whilst other more whimsical minds thought it an Aztec burial mound composed of sacrificed undergraduates. As often goes with the truth, the answer lies somewhere in between.

The Mound had indeed been started as a renaissance garden feature in the sixteenth century. However, 'the singular speed at which an Oxford college moves', as Robin Lane Fox, Garden Fellow, puts it, meant that it was barely completed by the Civil War. Oxford, much to its surprise, found itself at the centre of the maelstrom. The King was lodged at Christ Church, the Queen at Merton and the Privy Council at Oriel. The arsenal was piled high in the cloisters at New College, alongside artillery in the Magdalen deer park, whilst the students were being drilled on college lawns. All this for the very real threat of siege. Given New College's peripheral position on the city walls, Robert Pincke, the garden-mad Warden of New College, leapt at the opportunity to enlarge the existing garden Mound into a lookout post and cannon station; a spot where shivering students would stand,

steam rising from their breath, looking out over the fires of the enemy camp and wondering if they were on the right side of history.

Though he gets top marks for effort, Pincke's horticultural vision achieved little. The King slipped out of the city early one morning on 26 April 1646, and the somewhat delusional academic met his end not at the hands of a musket but by falling down the stairs. After the Civil War, the now enormous Mound returned to its original use as a Parnassus – a replica of the Greek mountain famed as home to the classical muses, sacred to Dionysus, god of wine.

Standing in front of the Mound today, this is not so hard to believe. Marooned amid acres of lawn, it seems more like a mysterious island than a viewing platform. Its tapering steps disappear up into *Quercus ilex*, or evergreen holm oaks, speaking of olive groves and the Aegean.

Placing my foot on the first step, an odd echo rang out. Some students playing a prank perhaps, or a muse, lurking high in the shadows,

The Mound | 29

answering back? Further up the stairs, a canopy arches overhead and I became engulfed in a darker space where the air is bittersweet with rosemary. Tripping on the final step, I fell onto the summit where, much to my disappointment, there were no muses, only a half-empty can of Carlsberg – how the muses have fallen.

Or not? Since its construction, an appropriately Dionysian spirit has presided over the Mound, illustrated by a recent discovery of seventeenth-century mugs, pipes and a bottle, as well as the bones of a lamb that asphyxiated on a Mars bar – testament to both the consistency, and ingenuity, of student interests. Today, the same spirit prevails, scene to many a ball, exploit, initiation and forfeit, with those performing badly at pool being made to run a trousers-down lap of the perimeter. Indeed, the college's recent proposal to trim the Mound's shrubbery resulted in public outcry, with scandalised articles in the London press accusing it of attempting to sabotage student love life – including one by an eminent economist, who was said to have used it to test the laws of supply and demand.

As I returned to the park-and-ride, it comforted me to think that students might be ensconced at the top of the Mound that very night. Here, they would be asking the same questions, and enjoying the same drunken conversation that their forebears had three hundred years before; talking, as Wykeham put it in his guide to college conversation, of 'songs and other honest solaces … poems, chronicles of kingdoms and the wonders of the world'. The only difference today being news of Professor Lane Fox's latest antics on the garden committee and tales of what happened the night before. As Andrew Marvel puts it in his poem 'The Garden':

Meanwhile the mind, from pleasure less,
Withdraws into its happiness;
The mind, that ocean where each kind

30 | *Follies*

Does straight its own resemblance find,
Yet it creates, transcending these,
Far other worlds, and other seas;
Annihilating all that's made
To a green thought in a green shade.

If there is such a thing as 'the genius of Oxford', then that is it.

Among the students that visited the Mound after its completion in the 1640s, a likely visitor was a Commoner of Wadham College, notable for his interest in stargazing and astronomy, for which the Mound was well suited. The student's name was Christopher Wren. Little did the young physicist know that his name was to become synonymous not only with architecture, but the Restoration of Charles II in 1660 and the flowering of his capital – to which my next site belongs.

On 27 August 1666, fresh from a tour of Paris, where he was allowed to peruse the drawings of Bernini, Wren submitted the first design of a dome for St Paul's Cathedral. A week later, he awoke with a start to be told that London was on fire. It is interesting to ponder what he must have thought on learning this. Sitting up in bed, momentary shock, concern for friends and relatives, perhaps, before realising that this was the defining moment of his life. Once the twenty-two 'Fire Judges', whose portraits, swathed in crimson and ermine, still hang in Lincoln's Inn today, had attempted to restore property after the fire, Wren was tasked with rebuilding much of the city. Besides his series of unbuilt plazas, the 'lost city', perhaps Wren's biggest contribution to the rebuilding of London was not St Paul's Cathedral, the Royal Hospitals and Palaces, but rather the fifty-one new city churches he designed to replace the eighty-seven that were destroyed. Among these was Christ Church Greyfriars, resting place of the wives of both Edward I and II, as well as favoured by 'Dick' Wittington, the celebrated fifteenth-century Mayor of London.

Passing through the modern City of London, a thicket of glass and steel, I craned my neck for Wren's masterpiece. A bus gave way and there it was: a majestic confection of crisp Portland Stone gleaming white against the grey offices that surround it. In spite of its moderate size, the spire seemed to dwarf everything around it, radiating the same supreme confidence that personified Restoration London. Much to the irritation of my fellow pavement warriors, I stopped to take it in: a square belfry, faced with twenty pilasters, rising to eight scrolls that unfurl into four sloping semi-circular pediments, topped with flaming pineapples – a symbol of welcome. These give way to a balustrade out of which rears an Ionic tempietto, topped with twelve urns, from which soars a Corinthian cupola, crowned with a golden onion dome.

The only word to describe it is baroque. After a miserable thirty years of Civil War, puritanism, plague and fire, it represents London's apotheosis as a European capital. It is as though a piece of St Petersburg, Paris or Rome had erupted through the earth, showering the sophisticated *joie de vivre* epitomised by the new monarch and his rakish court who, only a few years before, had processed through the streets as strangers from the Hague. For those arriving from the Thames, the churches, with their light, airy interiors below, focused on the spoken word, and sugary spires above, mirrored fifty times across the London skyline, must have presented London as the new Protestant Venice. A democratic city of sky follies bursting with new life, from the theatres to the printing presses and coffee houses, where Wren could be heard trying to outwit his newly formed Royal Society pals with his famous quip: 'the secret of architectural excellence is to translate the proportions of a dachshund into bricks, mortar and marble'.

I crossed the road and made for the Church. I was in for a shock. In the place of the elegant marble interior that I had been expecting was the blackened carcass of a church and a small public garden. Whipping out my phone, I quickly realised my error. Christ Church Greyfriars had fallen victim not only to the Great Fire of London, but also the Second Great Fire of London, which took place on 29 December 1940, one of the heaviest nights of the Blitz that claimed seven other Wren churches. Unlike the nearby St Paul's, Christ Church Greyfriars did not have a small army of bucket-bearers on the roof, and was obliterated. Apart from the spire and a font cover, saved by an unknown postman, only the garden remains, laid out in the same order as the old aisle and pews.

Wandering around the garden, I tried to take myself back to those awful nights where descriptions for one could be easily interchanged with the other. The shouts and screams of those still in the streets, or worse, in the buildings. Shadows, tripping over each other on the pavement, desperately covering their heads from the enemy which, to quote John Dryden's *Annus Mirabilis* are like: 'dire comets, which have scourged the town'. These are fought only by the 'sword of light' in the flashes of gunpowder, unleashed by the King's men, in an attempt to break the flame's path, or the anti-aircraft searchlights combing the skies above for the Luftwaffe. In either event, it was a dismal scene, described by Daniel Defoe as 'this great and monstrous Thing, called London', or as WWII correspondent Ernie Pyle put it: 'the most hateful, most beautiful single scene I have ever known'.

Looking back to the garden, I couldn't help but feel a sense of pride. As written in *The Times*, shortly after the second fire:

> The time will come – much sooner than most of us to-day can visualise – when no trace of death from the air will be left in the streets of rebuilt London. At such a time the story of the Blitz may begin to seem unreal

34 | *Follies*

not only to visiting tourists but to a new generation of Londoners. It is the purpose of war memorials to remind posterity of the reality of the sacrifices upon which its apparent security has been built. These church ruins, we suggest, would do this with realism and gravity.

Indeed they do. Today, the spire – an evolutionary folly in much the same way as Walsingham – represents London's triumph in rising, Phoenix-like, from the soot-stained remains of Civil War, fire and Blitz. A city forged in fire which sits, as Dryden wrote:

Like a Maiden Queen, she will behold,
From her high Turrets, hourly Suitors come:
The East with Incense, and the West with Gold,
Will stand, like Suppliants, to receive her doom.

With the headquarters of Merrill Lynch, financial giant, and a thousand others trading on its doorstep, it seems that Dryden was right. To borrow a line from Wren's memorial, inscribed on a sphere of black marble beneath the dome of St Paul's: when looking for evidence of London's grit 'Reader, if you seek his monument – look around you'.

Whilst the English Baroque was undoubtedly spearheaded by Wren, it arguably reached its zenith not in the spires of London but in the houses and garden buildings of Sir John Vanbrugh, often regarded as Wren's heir. This is surprising because not only was Vanbrugh completely untrained as an architect, but he had already enjoyed several careers. He had been an outspoken playwright championing women's rights, a haphazard producer, soldier, sailor, spy for William of Orange,

The Temple of the Four Winds | 35

prisoner in the Bastille, doolally merchant for the East India Company and herald. When Vanbrugh schmoozed Castle Howard as his first commission, the largest architectural project in the country, now regarded as one of the finest and most iconic buildings in England, he left the establishment utterly agog. As midlife crises go, it was nothing short of genius.

Castle Howard lies in North Yorkshire, an imposing part of the world famous for its grand houses and even grander inhabitants. Speeding towards the North York Moors, the dales looming dark on the horizon, I was extremely excited. This was not because I had seen the house in *Brideshead Revisited*, the somewhat stale source of much of its fame today, but rather because of its legendary size and scale, arguably our most fluent domestic expression of the most dramatic period in European architecture. Cue the son of the Prime Minister Robert Walpole, Horace Walpole, who, on visiting the house in 1777, wrote:

> Nobody had informed me that I should at one view see a palace, a town, a fortified city, temples on high places, woods worthy of being each a metropolis of the Druids, vales connected to hills by other woods, the noblest lawn in the world fenced by half the horizon, and a mausoleum that would tempt one to be buried alive; in short I have seen gigantic places before, but never a sublime one.

As I got closer to the house, the road widened into a great avenue, and I felt as though I was on the cusp of some ancient kingdom, with every pollard whispering of its might. Turning a corner, I found myself looking down a vast vista punctuated by three landmarks, each more extraordinary than the last. The first was a heavily rusticated gate set in a crenellated wall. From here the ground took a steep incline to a second gate crowned not by a triumphal arch or pediment, but an enormous pyramid that directs the eye up, only to see the third feature framed beyond

36 | *Follies*

it: a gigantic obelisk. As the layers of outbuildings unfurled before me, it seemed that I was being cast not as visitor but invader.

Perhaps this is appropriate. On reaching the house, I felt like a lone Goth reaching the outer walls of Rome. The house was stupendous: a castle metamorphosed into a palace, or palace into citadel; a playful manipulation of massing, projection and recession rising to an energetic skyline teeming not with soldiers but statues, cupolas and urns, all over-looked by a slender dome, topped with a glittering lantern. In a word, it is fantastic. In several more, it is powerful but delicate, English yet somehow foreign: a theatrical, even exotic building that is as much the result of an architect as a comedian who would, as Jonathan Swift wrote, 'build by

The Temple of the Four Winds | 37

Verse … and make my Muse the Architect'. In spite of its magnificence, however, this was not what I had come to see. Instead, I went to find a guide to take me to the most famous of Vanbrugh's garden buildings, the Temple of the Four Winds, which lies to the east of the house.

A few minutes later, guide successfully hijacked, I found myself on a path flanked by classical statuary that wound round the side of Ray Wood. This was the remains of the track that passed through the old village of Henderskelfe that was removed, in a typically bludgeoning eighteenth-century fashion, to make way for the house.

The further down the path I went, the more odd I felt. It was as though the moment I turned my back, the statues would hop off their plinths and scurry back into the woods. This feeling was perhaps because the gardens of Castle Howard were in many ways conceived as a theatre set; designed at the time of a paradigm shift in landscaping towards a style that aimed to recreate the shapeshifting worlds of Poussin and Lorrain. In other words, here the folly is no longer an isolated piece of art but part of a work of total-art that encompasses the entire garden. Eyes peeled for fornicating nymphs, I pressed on.

Finally, I saw the temple framed at the end of the walk, commanding a magnificent view out across the Howardian Hills. At a glance, it looked like a miniature version of Palladio's Villa Rotonda, on which Vanbrugh based the design. But on looking again, it seemed uncannily like a classical rendition of a Jacobethan pavilion, a fragment of The Globe, or even a Mughal dome. A shapeshifting folly – surely not? I then remembered what the later neoclassical architect Sir John Soane said of Vanbrugh: that he was 'the Shakespeare of architects'. Just as Shakespeare played around with a still molten language to revolutionise English theatre, so too did Vanbrugh with architectural elements – based on his own experiences – to create a new national Baroque that was distinct from its Catholic European counterparts.

In this sense, the Temple of the Four Winds can be read as a form of biography of Vanbrugh, as well as a sort of architectural manifesto – developed in healthy competition with Nicholas Hawksmoor. At its base, the temple is supported by a wide terrace that juts out in front of each of the pediments. With the lead Sibyls that flank the stair, the arrangement looks distinctly like a stage. It is as though Vanbrugh's most famous character, the try-hard rake Lord Foppington, might totter round the corner at any moment and declare his love for one of them – before being roundly rebuked. Above this are a pair of sash windows and a glazed door beneath a pediment. These only occupy around half the façade, the rest of which is blank, lending the building a masculine, almost fortified appearance, whilst the plethora of urns on the roof and pediments recall a Jacobethan roofscape.

Most curious of all though is the dome. With its ball finial, horizontal ribbing and heavy cornice, it reminds me of a Mughal *chhatri* – an Indian garden pavilion. In light of new research by Robert Williams, this isn't so hard to believe. When in Surat with the East India Company, Vanbrugh is known to have visited and sketched the local mausolea and palace architecture. This had reached its stylistic zenith in the completion of the Taj Mahal only thirty years before. It is not such a leap, then, to suppose that when designing a garden temple, Vanbrugh could have taken inspiration from the Mughal equivalent. A style that was famed not only for its delicacy, shadow and distribution of mass but similarly Elysian setting, thick with fountains and citrus trees. In this sense, the temple is indeed a meeting of the winds.

And there is more. For the temple's elaborate interior, designed for reading and drinking, recalls the final and perhaps most important aspect of Vanbrugh's life: his membership of the Kit-Cat Club, from which he gained the commission for Castle Howard. This was a prestigious group of wits joined by their avid belief in Whig policy: the pursuit of parliamentary democracy, a Protestant succession and resistance to a tyrannical French king, as well as the deposition of James II. They met to discuss these topics at the Trumpet Tavern in London, legendary for its mutton pies, or Kit Cats, after which the club was named. If Vanbrugh's design philosophy could ever be summarised, it would be the championing of these values.

Gazing at the temple's grimacing emperors, couched in gilded plasterwork and framed by cool, black scagliola columns, I wondered what they had seen – whether the Kit Cat Club had ever met there, or in similar places? What a glittering scene this would have been: the writers William Congreve and Joseph Addison, wigs askew, discussing the latter's new publication *The Spectator* in a corner, whilst aesthetes Lords Burlington and Cobham sketch plans for their gardens on a napkin in another. In the centre of the room, the bullish Prime Minister, Robert Walpole, roars with laughter, glass raised in an elaborate toast to liberty or some lover, in turn sketched by the painter Godfrey Kneller in preparation for his next club portrait. Outside, the elderly philosopher John Locke, forever perturbed, looks out at the half-built mausoleum, pondering the questions that those inside would rather not consider.

Before walking back to the house, I asked my long-suffering guide a final question: what did she think about all this? Her response: 'The mind boggles.' In the case of Castle Howard, it really does.

40 | *Follies*

After the rigours of Castle Howard, I retreated to Masham. The following morning, nestled in a corner of the King's Head, I tried to work out my next destination. This was difficult as Yorkshire is teeming with follies. To the east was Duncombe Park, famous for its Folly Walk that looks down onto the carcass of Rievaulx Abbey, as though from the heavens to a fallen earth. Whilst to the south is the legendary Fountains Abbey, whose tower looms out of the valley like the mast of some vast sunken ship, its ghostly windows like gun ports from which the psalms were blasted.

I opted for neither, instead going for Needle's Eye, a folly once attached to Wentworth Woodhouse, another Whig house. This lies seventy miles away so, diving into my car, I skidded out of the town and headed south. A couple of hours later, I pulled into a lane in the middle of nowhere. According to Google Maps, I was at Needle's Eye. This was disputed, however, by a large sign announcing 'Cortonwood Retail Park'. Cursing technology, I left the car and begin to comb the countryside in the pouring rain using my now attuned 'follydar'. I felt close to giving up when, at last, I saw an urn sticking out of the hedge. Crawling through this, I found myself in an empty field, face to face with what looks like a giant paperweight: an eerie stone pyramid, now green, topped with a flaming urn. Most notable of all, however, is the oddly pointed arch through its middle, as though from the Levant, now thick with foxgloves and cow parsley.

Even odder than this lonely, disembodied building is the story attached to it. This has many variations, but broadly they agree that one night – the date is disputed – the owner of Wentworth Woodhouse made a bet with a friend that he could drive a coach and horses through the eye of a needle, thus challenging the biblical quotation: 'It is easier for a camel to go through the eye of a needle than for a rich man to enter into the kingdom of heaven.' The following morning, realising his folly, the owner conceived the idea of a giant needle, perhaps with a

Middle Eastern arch, through which he could drive a coach and horses. This he duly did, thus proving the second part of the quotation: 'The things which are impossible with men are possible with God.'

Indeed, there was something godly about the owners of Wentworth Woodhouse: a titanic house which, with its 365 rooms and a 606-foot frontage — twice the length of Buckingham Palace — makes it the longest house in England. It was largely built by the second Marquess of Rockingham, Charles Watson-Wentworth, twice Prime Minister, famous for fighting the Jacobites aged fifteen, his outspoken criticism of government policy in America and racing five geese from Norwich to London for a bet. In

42 | *Follies*

order to consolidate power, Rockingham needed a base to compete with Houghton Hall in Norfolk, the home of his rival, Robert Walpole.

Thus, Wentworth Woodhouse was born: a Whig colossus, or cathedral, frequent venue to over a thousand guests and many royal events. Visitors would be led through the many-pillared lower hall, up a sweeping staircase and into the grand saloon, once dubbed the finest Georgian room in England – a great accolade for a generation of builders. In this magnificent double height space, sixty feet long and forty feet high, a marble floor radiated out in all directions, past paintings by Van Dyck and Stubbs, a state dining room where guests were fed from the fish ponds beneath the house, or bison from the park, and off into distant bedrooms. These had esoteric names such as 'The Village' or 'Blue Beard's Tower', and were so far away that guests would use confetti to find their way back to them. Such was its fame that Wentworth Woodhouse – and the Fitzwilliam family that inherited it – is thought to be the ensemble on which Jane Austen based Pemberley, home of the imperious Fitzwilliam Darcy in *Pride and Prejudice*. A house so impressive that it even tempts the unmaterialistic Elizabeth Bennet to 'reconsider' about its owner.

In the end, however, the strange folly on the hill came back to haunt the house. The wealth which had lent the Fitzwilliams such a god-like demeanour incurred the wrath of Manny Shinwell, the Labour Minister for Fuel and Power, who focused the eye of the post-war class storm on them. With the nationalisation of the coal mines in 1946, Shinwell ordered for mining to take place right up to the 'bloody front door' of the house – despite the University of Sheffield warning that the coal's quality was 'not worth the getting'. Local residents looked on with horror as the formal gardens were mangled and piled fifty foot high outside the Earl's bedroom. The local miners, who were devoted to the 'FitzBillies', even threatened to strike. Needless to say, this was futile. Two years later, Peter, the Earl, died in a plane crash. Finally, the Ministry of Health tried to requisition the house, its contents were sold and, rather than being blown up, it was turned into a school.

Today, Wentworth Woodhouse is a largely empty, soot-caked shell, threatened by subsidence. A recent push from the government, National Trust and Wentworth Woodhouse Preservation Trust, however, provides a glimmer of hope as they aim to turn the house back into a major hub for the local area – albeit in a different way to its previous incarnation. In this sense, Needle's Eye stands not only as a warning but also a memorial to the old Wentworth Woodhouse – perhaps the greater folly of the two. A house which, as the Latin motto: '*Mea Gloria Fides*' ('Faith is my Glory'), emblazoned across its gargantuan pediment suggests, needs all the help it can get.

y next destination is in rural Buckinghamshire, a county rich in architecture. Perhaps its two most famous sites are also its most contrasting: Stowe and Milton Keynes. They could not have fared more differently.

Ever since I was a child, I can remember the name 'Stowe', a place of almost mythical significance to any garden enthusiast. As a landscape experiment, Stowe trained and employed a who's who of designers: Vanbrugh, Bridgeman, Kent, Gibbs and Lancelot 'Capability' Brown, before changing the face of England, and indeed half the continental gardens from Paris to St Petersburg. For many, the landscape style developed at Stowe is considered England's greatest contribution to the visual arts.

Characteristically, it did not start in England, or even with Lord Cobham, the owner of the house, but instead with his friend, another member of the Kit Cat Club, Lord Burlington: 'the architect Earl'.

44 | *Follies*

When on his 'Grand Tour', Burlington made two discoveries. First, the buildings of Palladio. Second, a talented young designer called William Kent, who had escaped Yorkshire to live it up in Italy. Kent, or 'Kentino' to his Italian friends, was meant to be learning how to paint. Unfortunately, he was an atrocious painter – even Walpole admitted he was 'below mediocrity' – and so instead worked at procuring objects of art for the clueless English '*milordi*' to present to their parents at home. Bound by their similar interests and the latter's friendly, pragmatic manner, Kent and Burlington became lifelong friends and possibly lovers – a relationship that would not only revolutionise England's gardens but many of our greatest houses and interiors.

On returning to England, Burlington set Kent to work on his new villa at Chiswick, transforming his 'Palladian' dreams into a reality. At Chiswick, Kent was not only able to flex his creative muscles but got to know the most famous poet of the day, Alexander Pope – the English Voltaire – as well as the composer George Frideric Handel, also patronised by Burlington. The four became firm friends. As Pope wrote to his friend Martha Blount: 'we are to walk, ride, ramble, dine, drink, & Lye together. His gardens are delightful! his musick ravishing'. They must have presented an extraordinary sight: Burlington, quiet and scholarly; Kent, a bon viveur; Pope, only four foot six with a Great Dane called Bounce; and Handel, with a thick German accent.

During this time, Pope and Kent found a mutual love of gardening. The atmosphere must have been electric: Pope brimming with ideas of a looser style from the classical poems he had translated, Kent with practical experience of the landscapes in which they were written. It would prove a formidable combination.

In 1730, after a dry run at Chiswick, Kent was invited to apply these ideas at Stowe, resulting in what is now the most celebrated part of the garden: The Elysian Fields, in which we find my next site.

The Temple of British Worthies | 45

Given its Disneyland title, you could be forgiven for being sceptical about 'The Elysian Fields'. Fortunately, it does not disappoint. My immediate impression was that I had wandered into an impossibly beautiful corner of the countryside with swooping contours, emerald-green turf and the perfect number of trees. This, however, was quickly dispelled by the sight of the Temple of Ancient Virtue. Though not my chosen folly for this entry, there is something deeply meditative about the temple. Its sun baked walls not only radiate warmth but enjoy a restful synergy with their surroundings. Wherever I looked, the temple seemed to follow me: vistas snatched over a bush, behind a tree or sparkling in the water below. Rather than being led through a passive formal landscape, it is as though I was stumbling through an informal one that was actively metamorphosing around me, like a 3D equation, a classical painting or a poem, pinned together by its follies.

It is because of their aesthetic serendipity – a word coined by Walpole – that these landscapes, masquerading as virgin countryside, are considered gardens. When Kent arrived at Stowe, he took the reins from Charles Bridgeman, hitherto England's foremost gardener, who had begun the 'naturalisation' of gardens using the ha-ha, winding paths and garden buildings in conjunction with more formal avenues and parterres. Kent's genius lay in combining these newer elements with an incredible sense of rhythm. In the same way that he created enfilades in his interiors, or stacked furniture one above the other, so too did he create a series of interlinked spaces in his gardens, each with their own distinct character. As the ever-opinionated Walpole wrote, Kent was:

born with a genius to strike out a great system from the twilight of imperfect essays. He lept the fence, and saw that all nature was a garden. He felt the delicious contrast of hill and valley changing imperceptibly into each other, tasted the beauty of the gentle swell, or concave scoop.

Kent did not do this alone. Many see his sequential use of space as the fruition of his friendship with Pope. To this extent, Kent's gardens owe as much to paintings as they do the imaginary world of poetry. As Kent's pupil, the legendary Capability Brown, said when designing a garden: 'Now, there I make a comma; and there, where a more decided turn is proper, I make a colon: at another part (where an interruption is desirable to break the view), a parenthesis – now a full stop; and then I begin another subject.' This is perhaps best explained through Pope's *Epistle to Lord Burlington,* a kind of landscape manifesto, where he explicitly mentions Stowe itself. He writes:

in all, let Nature never be forgot
… let not each beauty ev'ry where be spy'd,
Where half the skill is decently to hide.

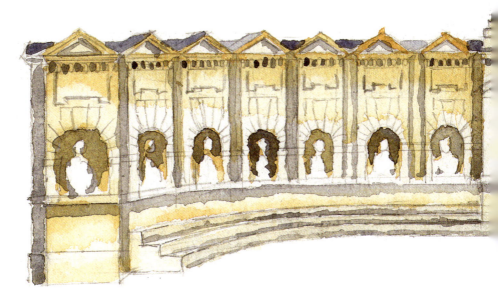

He gains all points who pleasingly confounds
Surprises, varies, and conceals the Bounds.
Consult the Genius of the Place in all;
… Nature shall join you, Time shall make it grow
A Work to wonder at – perhaps a STOWE

As we move through this bristling thicket of lines, the eye skipping from rhyme to rhyme, as though each a vista, Pope makes a number of profound points. First, that this new type of gardening is based not on taming nature but improving it – coaxing out 'the genius of the place'. Second, that the design process is synonymous with constructing verse or painting a picture. And third, that the effect relies on differentiation and harmony.

Ultimately, the ideas underpinning these poems, and thus The Elysian Fields, were political. Just as Vanbrugh sought a new Baroque to differentiate England from its autocratic neighbours, so too did land-owners seek a more relaxed style. Not only would this reflect England's

Follies

status as a mercantile democracy, but its shift from The Renaissance to The Enlightenment, where man no longer needed to visibly 'dominate' nature. Nowhere is this philosophy better illustrated than in the Temple of British Worthies, a folly which acts more as a summary than a standalone piece. This is an odd quasi-amphitheatre that sits opposite the Temple of Ancient Virtue across what is meant to be the River Styx. With no hooded boatman in sight, nor three-headed dog to dissuade me, I tramped back round the garden to take a closer look.

The temple, based on the Nymphaeum at the Villa Barbaro, consists of sixteen niches fanning out around a statue of Mercury, each containing a bust. Those on the left are men of ideas, those on the right are seven men and one woman of action. Lord Cobham considered each of these figures to have contributed to the development of a Whig England; a country whose solid Saxon heritage resonated with the liberties of Rome, whilst paradoxically contrasting its imperial tyranny.

Staring at the busts, I couldn't help but find them amusing. Standouts include Thomas Gresham, tired of explaining who he is, a terrified Milton next to a louche-looking Shakespeare, before a characteristically morose John Locke, whilst to the right is a smirking Black Prince, haughty Elizabeth, Walter Raleigh on the verge of a sneeze, a constipated Francis Drake and, around the corner, a deeply awkward looking John Barnard. Indeed, the latter was only chosen because of his opposition to Robert Walpole – with whom Lord Cobham fell out spectacularly – and he seems to know it. To quote David McKie: 'to come across Barnard in such illustrious company is as jolting as finding … Alan Titchmarsh flanked by Capability Brown and Gertrude Jekyll in a pantheon of gardening virtuosos'. He is, in other words, the classical equivalent of Richard Curtis's ubiquitous 'Bernard'.

Nevertheless, there is something strangely touching about this satirical gaggle of reprobates, who gaze longingly over the Styx and up into the heavens. I like to imagine that once the garden is closed, and the army of children have stopped poking their eyes, that the garden is populated not by nymphs but the busts; that their heavy eyelids blink open, their mouths open to the cool evening air, and Drake can finally relieve himself. Then, after briefly gossiping about the day's visitors, they continue to debate the great questions – as well as centuries of mocking Barnard. These conversations may be accompanied by the odd convivial 'yap', for at the back of the temple, Kent reveals that it is as much a monument to the great and good as it is to 'Signor Fido, an Italian of good Extraction', and Cobham's best friend: his dog. Indeed, poetry, paintings and politics aside, if Stowe could ever be summarised, it would be 'a memorial to friendship'. To quote Horace Walpole: 'Mahomet imagined an Elysium, Kent created many.'

hilst Kent is most famous as a landscape gardener, he was also a gifted architect. This is perhaps most evident in his design of the Horse Guards in London, the riot of stairs at 44 Berkley Square or the Marble Hall at Holkham. In such dynamic spaces, you get a sense of Kent as a 'total designer' whose work spanned everything from buildings, furniture and interiors to theatre backgrounds, state barges, tableware and uniforms. Swap diamonds for lashings of gilt, formaldehyde for plaster mouldings, and you have in Kent the Damien Hirst of the eighteenth century – another Yorkshire star.

Unlike Hirst, Kent was not cool but camp, exuding the same sense of fun and colour as his flamboyant schemes. Given his political neutrality, as well as the well-connected Burlington's keenness to entrench Palladianism as the national style, Kent was a deft social operator who had no trouble in gaining work. This caused long-term rival, William

50 | *Follies*

Hogarth, to nickname him 'KNT' – pun intended. Having literally moved in with the owners of whichever schloss he was improving, Kent, sporting a crimson turban, would breathe something of the Mediterranean back into the lives of his now world-weary patrons who, bored of draining their boggy acres, were keen to build palaces in which to display the treasures collected in their teens.

One of these patrons was the Duke of Beaufort, for whom Kent designed possibly the most elegant folly in England, Worcester Lodge, in 1746. This proves much more difficult to visit than the majority of sites for, unlike most follies, Worcester Lodge is still in possession of its hermit. The prospect of my impending grilling by a genuine hermit, or of bumping into the Duke himself, made me rather nervous. Indeed this is not any old duke but a descendent of John of Gaunt, whose hall was arguably the birthplace of badminton, who also acts as lead singer in his own band, 'The Listening Device' – their latest album, *Visions of Imaginary Furniture*, was released in 2017.

Clattering over the cobbles into Badminton's imposing courtyard, it transpired my challenge was not small talk with the self-proclaimed 'rock god' duke but finding Worcester Lodge, which was nowhere to be seen. After wandering around for an hour, I bumped into a groom. On asking the whereabouts of the lodge, he looked at me quizzically, before pointing down an avenue. There it was, three miles away: a dove grey smudge hovering pale on the horizon, like a cloud trapped in the trees.

And so began an epic walk that funneled me down the green corridor where the lodge morphed from smudge to silhouette, silhouette to outline, outline to form – whilst the house did the reverse behind me. The further I walked, the more it seemed I was witnessing a power shift where the landscape was dominated not by the house but the folly, for whom the house now served as an eye catcher – a distant speck of reality in a world of mirth.

Despite its exacting Palladian proportions, there is something fun

about Worcester Lodge. A rusticated base rises to a creamy façade at the centre of which is a semi-circular sash window, crowned with a pediment and blue saucer dome. This is flanked by symmetrical wings that connect to two pavilions featuring the same sash windows, topped with globe finials and pyramids. The result is wonderfully deceptive. Whilst it seems simple, the design is fantastically complex: a giant triangle formed of rectangles set with circles, through which you can see the sky, lending the building a light, airy quality, as much a feature of the park as it is the ether. In all, it is the apotheosis of Kent's architectural career. A building where he finally lets his hair down and pours a little panache into this otherwise imported style, making it his own in the same way that Vanbrugh did the baroque.

After ringing the bell, a side door creaked open to reveal a very small woman with sparkling eyes, white hair and a wide crooked smile.

52 | *Follies*

'You must be Rory. I'm the hermit – would you like some tea?'

After passing through a cool stone hall with a cantilevered stair that sweeps up to the first floor, we entered the dining room. This is entirely white except for the great shards of light which ripple across the plasterwork, causing its frosted bunches of grapes, roses, wheat and ivy to sparkle. This effect is then amplified by the space's inherent contrasts: it has the definition of an exterior but is an interior, seems baroque but is Palladian, is tethered to the ground but seems to be floating above the landscape. It feels, in other words, like walking inside a Viennetta.

A few minutes later, the hermit had magically produced some fine china cups and a delicious fruit cake that we enjoyed before a roaring fire. It was a ducal spread. Between mouthfuls of cake and a drop of whisky, she told me about how the Lodge was built as a banqueting house. Here, suspended above ground, he would use the space as a frame for magnificent meals in which to enchant society and compete with his contemporaries.

Several nips of whisky later, she offered to take me on a tour. First, of her sitting room, crammed with books on Pope, Burlington and Kent, before climbing down into the cellar where she produced a candelabra – 'the only way to see it', she asserted. Finally, talking about how the field outside was used for meetings of the local hunt, or how people kept dying in the ha-ha, she led me back up to the first floor where she opened a secret panel in the huge semi-circular window. Stepping onto the balcony, it seemed we were hovering above a giant map of the estate. Avenues radiated out in three directions, whilst the setting sun threw a shaft of golden light back up the central avenue, gilding the façade of which I was now a feature. The effect was mesmerising.

Reluctantly, I gathered my things to walk down the avenue and back into reality. Outside the lodge I bumped into an American tourist. Turning to me, he asked: 'Is this the Wooster Lodge?'

'It is,' I responded.

'Jeez, you don't get this in Texas.'

Though only half an hour away, my next site belongs to a very different landscape, where wold turns to combe in which, hidden away, we find the legendary city of Aqua Sulis, Aquamania or Baðum – otherwise known as Bath: England's Venice. Usually I am wary of such comparisons. To paraphrase Betjeman: perhaps it's best not to call Weymouth the Naples of Dorset. How many Italians call Naples the Weymouth of Italy? But in this case, I think its justified. Like Venice, Bath is a party city with serious Roman heritage, a replica of the Rialto Bridge and a complex series of canals. Unlike Venice, these were not for the transit of people but stone quarried by Ralph Allen, spearheading our next batch of businessman who, seeing the increasing popularity of Bath's natural springs, made a fortune providing the material out of which much of the city is built.

In order to advertise the stone, Allen built Prior Park on the outskirts of Bath, a magnificent house – the eighteenth-century answer to Gooding's Freston Tower – with perhaps the best folly bridge in England. This was built by John Wood, the same architect who built much of Bath. Though seemingly another Palladian architect, Woods went a step further than his contemporaries in the dubious 'classicism = British' (actually) debate, representing the ongoing interest in Ancient Britain. Instead, he claimed that the British King Bladud, a descendant of a Trojan Prince, had spent eleven years as a disciple of Pythagoras in Athens, where he contracted leprosy. On return to England, this was then cured by the waters of Bath, on which he built a city: The Metropolitan Seat of the Druids. Supposedly this stretched from modern Bath to the standing

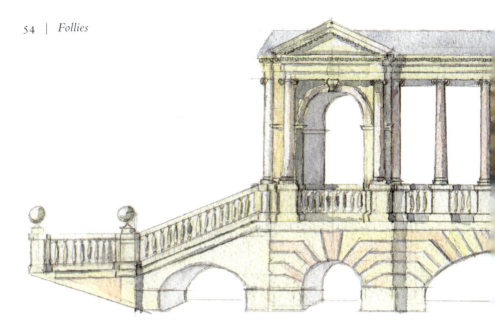

stones at Stanton Drew – somehow based on the Temple at Jerusalem – making it roughly the size of ancient Babylon, brimming with Druids, Greeks and Britons. Though a metropolitan Druid mincing around a classical plaza is hard to believe, the myth does go some way to explaining the popularity of Bath, considering how disgusting its water is.

Having parked my car on a hill, I began to tramp my way up to the house. This is spectacular: a vast villa of golden, sun-kissed stone, flanked by two wings that fan out around it, as though an amphitheatre for which the audience were Allen's many guests. They were an impressive line-up: the writer Henry Fielding, actor David Garrick, politician Pitt the Elder, as well as our old friend Pope. Characteristically, the latter had a hand in crafting the landscape which, as I turned to face the view, rendered me momentarily speechless.

Below me, a scoop of green swept down to the valley bottom where, framed by trees, I could see the distant outline of a bridge floating over a lake. Beyond this, instead of the sea described in Fielding's fictional

description of the house, lay the swirling streets of Bath, whose crescents foam not with water but avenues, gardens and parks. As one equally amazed visitor quipped in 1788, it is 'a noble seat which sees all Bath, and which was built for all Bath to see'. In other words, for a city of boulevardiers, the one is constantly posing for the other.

The more I took in the view, the more I realised that its composition relies entirely on the bridge. For it is this, like a pin, that ties together the ensemble, drawing the eye down and forcing it to register the drama of the natural landscape, without which it would simply unravel. Curious, I made my way down the combe which, interspersed with ski-pole-wielding couples, strangely resembled a glacier. This is divided into three chambers. First, the immediate field where the trees funnel outwards, like a 3D conical flask. After this, the trees recede and the saddle of earth gives way to create an enormous delta, dusted with buttercups, that seems to be in the middle of the countryside. Finally, you pass through a small gate and arrive in a much more intimate setting, where the trees have risen up to obscure the city, placing all focus on the bridge before you.

The Palladian Bridge is one of the most famous examples of English 'aquatecture'. One of three such designs, the other two residing at Wilton Park and Stowe – with a fourth in St Petersburg. Unlike other versions, however, the bridge at Prior Park is entirely ornamental, a ridiculously elaborate structure for such a small lake. But this does not detract from its beauty: an exquisite arrangement of arches, pediments and columns, all in the finest Bath stone that has turned from white to mottled peach. This is reflected in the mirror-like pool below, as though a bridge in another world for which we are the submerged party. Given its incongruity, if you were to stumble across the Bridge, you could be forgiven for thinking that it was indeed the remnant of another age. To quote 'The Ruin', a fragmentary Anglo-Saxon poem about a lone Saxon coming across the city's ruined baths:

> The halls of the city
> Once were bright: there were many bath-houses,
> A lofty treasury of peaked roofs, many troop-roads, many mead-
> halls
> Filled with human-joys until that terrible chance changed all that.
> … countless heated streams … until the ringed pool
> Hot … where there were baths
> Then is … That is a kingly thing—
> A house …
> A city.

Walking beyond the bridge and looking back, I saw that the construction is not a bridge after all but rather an aquatic ha-ha designed to distract the eye from the drop in water level. To this extent, the bridge

The Palladian Bridge | 57

is not a crossing over a body of water at all but rather a screen or threshold between the rural and the urban: an aquatic folly metaphorically crossing over into the folly spa town beyond.

fter Prior Park, I bombed half an hour down the road to the seat of the ultimate eighteenth-century Gooding – Henry Hoare, founder of Hoare's Bank, who made a fortune around the same time that Wren was rebuilding London. As with all good banking families, Henry had a son, another Henry, who built a country seat from which to boast his family's newfound wealth at Stourhead in Wiltshire. This was inherited by his son, Henry 'the Magnificent' who, as illustrated by both his name and portrait, resplendent in crimson waistcoat on a rearing stallion, lived life to the full. This was not to last. A year after Henry 'the Magnificent' married, his wife, Anne, died in childbirth, followed by his second wife, Susanna, as well as his children. Henry was devastated. Instead of taking to the bottle, or marrying yet again, however, Henry channelled his grief in an unusual way. With the help of Henry Flitcroft – another Burlington protégée – he cultivated one of the most beautiful and personal landscape gardens in England: a real Secret Garden.

Whilst not quite as famous as Stowe, Stourhead would certainly be on the Mayfair section of the garden Monopoly board. Nevertheless, as I drove into the National Trust car park, I was quietly unconvinced. How could an architectural amateur like Hoare be on a par with Kent, Brown, or Repton? Strolling through the pretty village that precedes the garden, I remained doubtful until, suddenly, the view expanded and I had to eat my words: before me was a view that looked uncannily like Claude Lorrain's painting of *Aeneas at Delos*. As a single composition, it was possibly the most impressive I had seen thus far. A bridge spans the

58 | *Follies*

entrance to a lake which stretches to the other side of the valley where, perching on the bank, is a replica of the Pantheon in Rome. The sun swept across the water and came to rest on the building, which shone ethereally through the morning mist. As James Lees-Milne wrote: 'see Stourhead, and die'. Clearly, I had underestimated Henry. On crossing the garden threshold, I came across an inscription from the *Aeneid* suggesting that he presumes as much: '*Procul, O Procul Este, Profani*' ('Keep away, oh keep away you who are profane!') Checking myself for profanity, and finding most of it spent on the National Trust parking metre, I pressed on.

At ground level are great thickets of rhododendrons, whilst above is a canopy of Spanish chestnut, Japanese acer, beech, tulip trees and maple. In the summer, these cast deep shadows over the path, whilst in autumn, a blaze of colour that fills the air with caramel. Deep within the garden, the path dips and you find yourself being led into a mossy underground lair: a grotto. Here, light spills down through a hole in the domed roof to reveal a round chamber with a floor of glittering pebbles. There is a murmur of water and the smell of damp rock.

To my left was a jagged window looking out over the lake, whilst to my right was a series of concentric niches. Thinking that was it, I hurried on before a flash of white caught my eye. Turning to my right, I saw, set deep within the niches, the body of a sleeping girl who seemed to glow in the darkness: a water nymph – or rather, an exceptionally lifelike statue of one. A bead of water dropped from the stalactites above and ran down my spine. I felt electrified and took it as a sign that, despite the stony visage, I was not entirely alone. As Henry wrote, the grotto is 'filled with fresh magic'. I thought about how, if a drunken reveller stumbled into the grotto to sober up, they might have turned to the niches only to find an empty bed where the nymph usually lies – before hearing a splash from the window, and wondering if they were drunker than they had realised.

The Temple of Apollo | 59

Beyond the grotto lies the Temple of Hercules – the aforementioned Pantheon. Here, 250 years before, I pictured Henry and his relations splayed beneath parasols, perhaps being entertained by the same Mr Garrick from Prior Park, one of the garden's many visitors. As Henry wrote: 'gracious what a Figure of Fun is here. Mr Garrick has not His fellow Private as well as Publick entertainment.' Nevertheless, whilst the temple is commonly seen as the high point of Stourhead, my destination lay deeper still within the garden.

In order to access it, I had to make a choice. I could either follow the easy path that runs flat by the water, or pass through a dank rubble arch with a steeper climb beyond it. Now something of an expert on eighteenth-century garden psychology, I chose the harder, more 'virtuous' option. The path was genuinely challenging. After twisting up a precarious rubble stair, I plunged into the darkness of an underground tunnel. What lay beyond it was worth every stumble. Emerging from the tunnel, I strode onto a grass plateau, high above the rest of the garden. At the end of this is The Temple of Apollo, copied from the ruins of Baalbek, 'The Sun City' in Syria.

Like the god after which it is named, there is something radiant about the temple: a domed cylindrical building of mottled gold, orbited by a scalloped entablature, as though shards of light from a glittering nimbus. On entering the building, you see a fairly plain interior. Take a couple of steps to the centre of the room, however, and you find the sound of your breath amplified a hundred-fold – as though a minotaur smarting behind you. Speak, and it is a thousand: a great, thundering sound that ricochets off the walls, as though the voice of Apollo himself. Naturally, this makes you look up, where your gaze is met by a miniaturisation of the building's exterior: a dazzling sunburst bathed in light, at the centre of which is a tiny face, as though that of a child, staring back down at you.

Resting on the steps of the temple, looking out over the lake, I felt extremely moved. The tiny face in the dome reminded me of what I'd learnt at the beginning of the garden: that Hoare brought paradise to Stourhead not only to remember his family but as a place in which he might imagine them, and thus remain close to them. It is no coincidence that on building a hermitage he wrote: 'I believe I shall put in to be myself The Hermit.' In this way, Stourhead is a real version of perhaps the most famous garden play: Tom Stoppard's *Arcadia*. It is a place where Henry, like the urbane Septimus, retreats into a garden as hermit in homage to those he has lost.

Moreover, just like the landscape in *Arcadia*, Stourhead is a transitional garden in the shift from reason to sensation: from a garden inspired by paintings to one that was itself painted. This change is best seen in the Temple of Apollo's sister building, a belvedere known as King Alfred's Tower, built a couple of miles from the garden on the spot where King Alfred is said to have raised the Saxon standard against the Vikings at the Battle of Ethandun (or Edington) in 878. (This is deeply ironic, as in 1944, a Canadian C-64A Norseman plane crashed into the tower, killing five actual soldiers – an architectural 'own goal' if ever there was one.)

After a bracing walk through the Wiltshire countryside, I was suddenly in a very different landscape. A broad avenue widened into a pasture filled with wildflowers. At the end of this loomed a gigantic tower, its sheer wall of brick frosted with lichen, casting it a hazy pink. It is more of an apparition than a building – the sort of structure that dredges up half-buried dreams, making you question the existence of wizards again or listen for the distant drone of a dragon.

There is something duplicitous about the tower. If the sun is out, it stands as another monument to 'Britishness', hailing the county of Saxon barrows, Stonehenge and the White Horse carved indelibly into the Downs. If the sun goes behind the clouds, however, it takes on a very different aspect, becoming dark and brooding: the picture of a Gothic folly. It is the materialisation of a new philosophy, summarised by Walpole, who writes that whilst 'one must have taste to be sensible to the beauties of Grecian architecture; one only wants passion to feel the Gothic'.

In this fantastical setting, Henry enjoyed playing with the children of his remaining family. As he wrote towards the end of his life: 'Thank God they are all fine & well & now make nothing of walking round the Gardens & I mounted the Tower Thursday with the Dear Children. They were vastly delighted with this spot.' Perhaps the most delighted was his grandson, Richard Colt Hoare who, as he grew up, increasingly enjoyed talking to his grandfather about the garden and finally inherited it from him on the latter's death. Henry was buried next to his father in the church at the entrance to the garden, and his epitaph serves as a wonderful summary of his creation. He was: 'Thankful [for] these fair &

flowery paths he trod, / And priz'd them only as they lead to GOD' – or rather, to his family. The garden was transitional in more than one way.

My next site was an example of how a folly hunt should be undertaken. After the rigours of Stourhead, I was invited for dinner with a friend's grandmother nearby. I was not entirely sure of the address, but I knew the area and thought I should be able to work it out as I went along. For those who don't know South Somerset, however, this was a classic 'grockle' error – local slang for a tourist. Though close, Wiltshire and South Somerset are geographically very different, the ancient border between Saxon Wessex and the Celtic Cornwall beyond. The former is an expanse of wide chalky plain – ideal for the nonchalant navigator – the latter an intimate rat run of lanes that would have made even Shackleton yearn for a vantage point. With no phone signal to speak of, Google Maps failed, and I got very, very lost.

After following the road down a decidedly eerie hollow, I finally evacuated the car near Barwick, with the intention of climbing a hill for some signal. As I did so, an odd structure growing out of the hedge-row on the horizon caught my eye. I decided to investigate. After battling through the cow parsley, I discovered a footpath which, much like the hollow, is sunken into the ground, as though an ancient thoroughfare. I followed it for about ten minutes until, quite suddenly, I was face to face with what is perhaps the weirdest folly in England, and one that I was more than familiar with: Jack the Treacle Eater.

Though I had read about this famous structure many times before, I had never considered it worth visiting. How wrong I was. At a glance, it looks like a wonky witch hat balanced on a rubble arch. On closer inspection, however, you notice that the

64 | *Follies*

cylinder is punctuated by a tiny door and then crowned with crenellations. These in turn taper into a ball finial on which balances the figure of Mercury springing into the sky. It is, in a word, bonkers. It is also extremely unnerving. The folly seems to have been built as a boundary marker or eye catcher to the nearby house – probably to relieve unemployment in the eighteenth century. Nevertheless, this can't be certain. In fact, nothing about it can be certain. The structure lacks any kind of name, date, or style to which it can be attributed, let alone a purpose. It is the thoroughbred of follies, a class of building that, to quote Gwyn Headley: 'impale themselves on the memory by their pointlessness'. To date, we have only two clues. First, that it hovers in the background of a mysterious eighteenth-century portrait. Second, that it is called 'Jack' after a local messenger who, fed on black treacle, would deliver messages to London for the local landowners.

But who was Jack? Why was he so special? And how on earth could he run to London? There was something a little strange about the whole thing.

With mist beginning to settle in the hollow, and dusk – or 'dimpsey' – setting in, I felt, for the first time since embarking on this journey, a little spooked. 'Jack' is not the sort of name you want to whisper alone in the dark on All Hallows Eve – known here as 'Punkie Night'. It is no coincidence that the protagonists of nearly every children's story bear his name: Jack Frost, Jack and Jill, Jack and the Beanstalk, Jack the Giant Killer and so on. A form of sprite, his name is synonymous not only with folklore but magic, the supernatural and superstition – an indigenous answer to the classical nymph or fawn. This is not because 'Jack' is evil per se but rather because of his reputation as a trickster. In Ireland, he is known as Stingy Jack;

Jack the Treacle Eater | 65

in the Welsh Marches as a wizard called Jack-o'-Kent, whilst in England and more generally, as grinning Jack-o'-lantern, made from hollowed-out pumpkins or mangel-wurzels. His doings are recorded in a myriad of tales, but perhaps the most common involves the Devil.

One day, Jack was visited by the Devil, who told him that his time on earth was up. Keen to buy time, Jack asked the Devil for a final pint at the pub. The Devil, being a genial fellow, agreed. Once at said pub, Jack asked the Devil to indulge him in one last piece of trickery: to transform himself into a coin with which to settle the bill. Again, the Devil agreed, and turned himself into a coin. Thereupon, Jack whipped the coin into his pocket, where he conveniently had a cross, thus trapping the Devil in the coin, to be released only once he had promised not to take Jack to hell. This the Devil did. Finally, Jack died of natural causes. Unfortunately, given his track record, he was unable to pass through the pearly gates. Keen not to get lonely, Jack asked the Devil if he might go back on his word, to which the answer was a smug 'no'. As such, Jack was thrown a hot coal and banished back to earth where he was doomed to roam the shadows as a conduit between good and evil, scaring children and generally being a nuisance.

66 | *Follies*

Nevertheless, Jack is not all bad. In Cornwall, he is known for killing the indigenous giants Gourmaillon, Bunderbore and Thunderdell, whilst in England, he also takes the form of Jack in the Green, a pagan fertility symbol associated with May Day. Indeed, the more you learn of Jack, the more you realise that he is not a specific person but rather the personification of an idea; an idea that has echoed through time and place, from 'Hans' in Germany to 'Ivan' in Russia, through children's books, folklore, fable and legend, first whispered in a lost Indo-European language in a country now as mythical as the tales conceived within it. It is no coincidence then that Mercury, the god at the top of the building, has many characteristics in common with Jack. Not only is he god of travellers, messages and boundaries but trickery, luck and thieves. He is essentially the Roman manifestation of the same 'cheeky chap' who, like the folly on which he stands, is not afraid to break the rules. In this sense, the arch is not a monument to a specific Jack but rather a gateway, boundary or even conduit to a more ancient part of England: a place where the memory of Jack still lingers.

Unexpectedly, my phone lit up with signal. To be on the safe side, I saluted the statue and hurried back to the car. As I did so, however, I was careful to go around the arch and not through it. You can never be too careful.

My next destination took me east to London. As I drove, I imagined two figures making the same journey on 2 March 1737: the young David Garrick, a Huguenot immigrant, and his old teacher Samuel Johnson, one hoping to act, the other to write. Little did they know that the former would become the most famous actor, the Kenneth Branagh of his day, and the latter the author of the first dictionary.

Once in London, the untrained Garrick worked for the family's ailing wine business. This gave him free rein to hang around the theatres and the Bedford Coffee House, an actors' haunt, where he was known for standing on a table and imitating other performers. Soon enough, he became an understudy and, when the opportunity to perform finally arose, he was an instant hit. As the now elderly Pope wrote on seeing Garrick: 'I am afraid the young man will be spoiled for he will have no competitor.' He amazed audiences with a naturalistic acting style that complimented the period's increasingly sentimental temperament, as well as helped to re-popularise the work of Shakespeare by reinterpreting it for a modern audience. So affecting was Garrick that Sir Joshua Reynolds is said to have taken three days to recover from his King Lear. He was also a comedian, famous for his role as a gouty old noble, Lord Chalkestone, who would peer down into the orchestra pit and shout: 'Upon my word, here's a fine ha-ha, and a most curious collection of every-green and shrubs!' Indeed, when he was not writing or acting, he would spend his time crawling through the Burlingtons' ha-ha, disguised as a woman, in order to woo Eva Maria Veigel, a Viennese dancer and ward of the Burlingtons, who disapproved of Garrick. Needless to say, the two married anyway.

Soon enough, Garrick had become a 'national treasure' with over 250 portraits of himself – more than the King. As Samuel Johnson wrote: the acting 'profession made him rich and he made his profession respectable'. The time had come to 'do a Gooding' and express his newfound success in stone – or rather stucco. This he duly did with the architect Robert Adam, an associate of Chambers, in a villa in Twickenham. With its neat red-brick terraces and abundant greenery, this was the 'Bloomsbury' of the eighteenth century, home not only to satirists Pope, Swift and Gay, but the painter Hogarth and Horace Walpole – who needs no introduction. As a borderline aristocrat, however, Garrick's new home was not complete without a folly. Thus Garrick decided to build a temple to Shakespeare, the man to whom he owed much of this success, and fill it with his things – including a chair carved from a mulberry tree supposedly planted by the Bard in Stratford-upon-Avon.

Hopping off the bus at 'Garrick Villa', I spied a suspiciously classical dome peeking up from a sunken garden on the other side of the road. Despite its proximity to the traffic, the garden is peaceful, with a sloping lawn that leads down to a magnificent sweep of the Thames, over which glides a steady stream of scullers – not unlike the boatmen of the eighteenth-century. It must be said that there is nothing even remotely Shakespearean about the folly which, at the end of the lawn, looks like a classical potting shed. But as potting sheds go, it's pretty wonderful and exactly as portrayed in Zoffany's famous portrait of the Garrick family: a vision of white and pink from which juts a varnished portico that shimmers next to the water. Like its owner, it has a certain undeniable presence.

Inside, this is amplified by an enormous statue of Shakespeare that looks suspiciously similar to Garrick, as well as copies of a number of the actor's portraits by Gainsborough, Reynolds, Hogarth, Zoffany and Batoni. In Hogarth's picture, he is a dainty Richard III, complete with ruff, doublet and wild Elizabethan hair. In Reynolds', he is a red-faced squire, dressed in crimson velvet and seated next to his wife, whilst in Gainsborough's depiction, he is a member of the literati with a cocked eyebrow, the flicker of a smile and a quizzical eye that follows you around the room. Like shards of a mirror, each of these present a glint of Garrick, from which you can try to build a complete picture of the man.

The more I stayed in the temple, the easier it was to imagine him in the room with me. Like his acting style, he seemed multifaceted. On the one hand, I imagined he was very serious, pacing the temple learning lines, pondering how to sort the latest theatrical spat or

Garrick's Temple to Shakespeare | 69

discussing Shakespeare late into the night with members of The Club – an intellectual gathering that featured writers Johnson and Boswell, and philosophers Adam and Burke. But on the other hand, he also seemed remarkably playful, entertaining friends on the lawn with his

70 | *Follies*

outlandish imitations and bird noises. For some, this was too much. As the snobbish Walpole – somehow still alive – growled: 'be on your guard; he's an actor'. But for others, this quiet spot in good company was heaven, causing Johnson to remark: 'Ah, David, it is the leaving of such places that makes a deathbed so terrible.'

Garrick's most appreciative audiences, however, were arguably not adults but children, whom he loved but was not blessed with himself. One friend recalled how 'he produced a thousand monkey tricks on me; he was a Punch, a Harlequin, a cat in the gutters, then King Lear with a mad touch'. Or another how she saw him entertaining a small boy who, enraptured, cried: 'Massa Garrick do so make me laugh. I shall die laughing!' Perhaps this is why Zoffany's portrait of the temple has a little boy hiding behind one of the columns, as though waiting for the motionless actor's next wink.

Today, the temple's function hasn't changed much. It is still used for thespian lectures and teas, as well as Shakespeare workshops for a number of local schools, filling it with children. Though perhaps not a place where we can picture Shakespeare himself, it is a place where, to quote his *Midsummer Night's Dream*:

> imagination bodies forth
> The forms of things unknown, the poet's pen
> Turns them to shapes and gives to airy nothing
> A local habitation and a name.

That name, of course, is Garrick – whose ability to do the same with Shakespeare, to channel his words and electrify them for modern audiences, is partly the reason we still read him today.

As I left the temple, I turned to one of the guides to thank her for her help, although commented it was a shame about the nearby road.

'Funny you should say that,' she responded, 'that's exactly what Samuel Johnson said.'

Even more Shakespearean than Garrick's folly, however, was a scene that unfolded just up the road in Kew Gardens: an elderly man, dressed in rags, howling at a great pagoda, before a flurry of men in neatly powdered wigs and crimson coats drag him away, screaming of his beloved folly. That man was, of course, the mad monarch, King George III.

Kew had long been popular with the royal family. In the medieval period, the kings would retreat to 'Keyho', a quiet haven south of the city – like a proto-Balmoral. Fresh from Germany, Kew proved useful to the fraught Hanoverian court as a place where George II could escape his domineering father and, in time, where George II's son, Frederick, 'the lost Prince of Wales', could do the same. In this leafy, cosmopolitan corner of London, Frederick's children, including the young George III, enjoyed a relatively normal upbringing. On sunny days, they would play rounders, ninepins and cricket – which their father adored – whilst any great man that came to visit their father would invariably be coerced into a play, with the latter accompanying them on his cello.

This, however, all came to an end one March in 1751, when Frederick contracted pneumonia after a day's gardening. On the death of her spouse, Frederick's widow, Augusta, turned – much like Henry Hoare at Stourhead – to the garden. This was already relatively famous owing to the additions made by her mother-in-law, Queen Charlotte, in 'Merlin's Cave', a Disneyland version of Stowe's British Worthies inhabited by a Rousseau-esque 'thresher poet' who was invariably caught at the pub. After being introduced to William Chambers, however, a young

72 | *Follies*

architect just back from China, the redoubtable Augusta took a slightly different approach. Not only did she found a botanic garden but hired Chambers to design a number of buildings in the latest 'exotic' style in which to drink the equally exotic stimulant 'tea'. The result was the most impressive, and realistic, pagoda outside China.

Having never been to China, I was particularly excited to see this folly. After a pleasant stroll through Richmond, a place which still retains much of the quiet gentility that made it so attractive to the royals, I soon arrived at the gardens. Walking down its great avenue, I envisaged what Kew must have been like: the princes charging around on wooden horses, the air sweet with freshly scythed grass and filled with the strange sound of zebra or Tartarian pheasants from their mother's menagerie. Finally, at the end of the avenue, the conifers swept back, like a fire curtain in a theatre, and I found myself in the eye of the East.

On first sight, the pagoda looks like the architectural manifestation of the trees around it; a giant conifer whose reddish, lacquered trunk tapers upwards, ribbed by a series of flared canopies: the underside crimson, the top a bluey green. When it was built, these would have been adorned with eighty gilded dragons painted with glass, as well as bells and a golden 'demon arrester' or finial, causing the building to either shimmer or sing, depending on the weather. The result is profoundly impressive: a taste of the Forbidden City in the English equivalent, an ancient form of architecture whose earliest examples are far older than people often realise – roughly contemporary with Hadrian's Wall. It is perhaps for this reason that local residents believed that the pagoda was not a pavilion at all but rather the elaborate home of a gryphon – half lion, half eagle – brought back by Captain Cook, whose progeny still haunt the site today.

As with most stylistic shifts, however, there is more to the pagoda than meets the eye. On visiting China – this time with the Swedish East India Company – Chambers was deeply impressed. This was not merely because of its dazzling colour. From a civic perspective, China's organisation was far beyond anything in Europe, with visitors frequently commenting on the quality of its roads – often paved with marble – the safety of its streets and its commercial orientation. Whilst aesthetically its looser gardening style, where man was not set apart as special but considered part of nature, provided a moral alternative to Kent's classical gardens and Brown's increasingly sterile deserts of green, void of any follies at all. This sophisticated urban model chimed with the increasingly socio-economic theory being churned out of Edinburgh which, with its gleaming New Town, the 'Athens of the North', was deemed the new powerhouse of the Enlightenment.

Though a flagrant example of cultural appropriation, Chambers' pagoda was built out of a genuine enthusiasm for Chinese culture, which he believed could provide direction for the ever-expanding, and increasingly dissolute, British Empire. He was determined not to produce yet another aesthetic 'halfpenny' – used by many of his contemporaries as a way of experimenting with one style in the name of another

74 | *Follies*

– but rather to 'put a stop to the extravagancies that daily appear under the name of the Chinese'. Apart from getting the number of floors wrong – it should be odd, as opposed to even, which brings bad luck – Chambers succeeded. Not only did this spark a new fashion that would, yet again, sweep Europe, it signalled the next lap in garden philosophy, the seeds of which we saw at Stourhead, where man is the creature of an omnipotent god to whom he should *feel* fear, awe and reverence – in other words, the sublime.

It was in the wake of this more natural outlook that George III, now king, brought up his vast brood of fifteen children as a model of respectability. As his continental equals became increasingly autocratic, retreating into their vast pleasure palaces, George did the reverse, taking care to keep Kew open to the public. Here he would be seen striding about the gardens, children in tow, shouting his characteristic 'What! What!' or 'Hey! Hey!', or offering kangaroo babies to nervous courtiers. When his gardeners finally protested, the King responded with the line: 'My subjects, sir, walk where they please.' Indeed, as great strides were made in science, industry and agriculture – often brought to Kew – the King took care to act as their patron, champion and student, earning him his oft quoted nickname 'Farmer George'. He was, in many ways, a model king.

It is for this reason that the King's descent into madness was so shocking – perhaps invoked by Chambers' numerical mistake in the pagoda's number of floors. Whilst George's life has been well documented, not least in Alan Bennett's magnificent play, *The Madness of King George III*, his continuing fascination with the pagoda has not. Why he ran to it is, of course, hard to say. Perhaps it was because the pagoda lay furthest from the palace? Or because it reminded him of his childhood? However, I like to think that the pagoda, with its sublime connotations, was the closest thing that George could find to solace: something equally as foreign, and indeed terrifying, as the thoughts that flashed across his mind, thus allowing him brief moments of lucidity. To this extent, perhaps it was the King himself who was the long-lost gryphon of Kew: a legendary creature, half man, half myth who, plucked from his native land, took comfort from the presence of another.

As I headed back to my car, through the great glasshouses, where mists filter down from the domes above, and every step constitutes another continent, I felt the same mix of awe and inspiration that George sought to encourage 250 years before. Fortunately, I didn't have to accept a baby kangaroo to experience it.

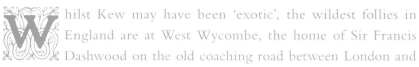hilst Kew may have been 'exotic', the wildest follies in England are at West Wycombe, the home of Sir Francis Dashwood on the old coaching road between London and Oxford. Today, West Wycombe is known largely as a set for films such as *The Importance of Being Earnest*, *Another Country*, *Belle* or, more recently, *Pride and Prejudice and Zombies*. In the eighteenth century, however, it was infamous, for not period dramas, but some of the greatest parties of the age set in gardens second only to Stowe. For a century of debauchery, this was no mean achievement.

Like many of his contemporaries, Dashwood's taste for flamboyance began on his Grand Tour. This was no continental jaunt but a dizzyingly exotic series of journeys to Rome, Russia, Ephesus, Smyrna, Palmyra, Baalbek, Giza and Constantinople. On these trips, accompanied by a humourless tutor, Dashwood not only developed a sophisticated taste in art but a reputation as an accomplished hellraiser – one that makes a Full Moon Party in Thailand today look like a trip to the local play centre. Known as the 'Chevalier' Dashwood, in Russia,

76 | *Follies*

he attempted to seduce the Tsarina by dressing as Charles XII. Whilst in Rome, he was expelled from the Papal States for deeds such as disguising himself as an obscenity-whispering cardinal, or stealing into a scourging ceremony at the Sistine Chapel dressed as a night watchman, before horsewhipping the nave.

Pranks aside, Dashwood took travelling seriously. As Benjamin Franklin later said of him, he who has been 'for many Years engaged in publick Affairs, seen all parts of Europe, and kept the best Company in the World, is himself the best exciting'. In 1732, in the cabin of a ship off Genoa, Dashwood and a number of friends established the Society of Dilettanti, a club designed to foster knowledge and appreciation of classical culture in England, where the president would dress in a toga and the secretary as Machiavelli. Though know-it-all Walpole dismissed the enterprise: 'the nominal qualification is having been in Italy and the real one being drunk; the two chiefs ... were seldom sober the whole time they were in Italy', it was a serious endeavour. Not only did the society send architects to the excavations at Herculaneum and Pompeii, it raised a subscription for the publication of *Antiquities in Athens*, a work that led to the subsequent neoclassical craze for 'Grecian Gusto'.

Back in England, Dashwood set about bringing this more advanced understanding of the classical world to Buckinghamshire. The ceilings of the house were painted with feasting gods, to replicate those in the Palazzo Farnese, whilst the walls were remodelled with swirling scagliola, as though one of the recently unearthed Roman villas. Most spectacular of all, however, was the addition of the West Portico, an austere pediment copied from the Temple of Bacchus, Ionia, that reflected the increasing popularity of a simpler Greek classicism, and also served as a transitional feature into the picturesque gardens below.

In September 1771, the portico was opened with typical Dashwoodian flair. After a banquet, the guests, dressed as 'Bacchanals,

Priests, Priestesses, Pan, Fauns, Satyrs, Silenus etc. all in proper habits & skins wreathed with vine leaves, ivy, oak' spilled out of the house's frescoed terraces and descended into the torchlit gardens below. Here, we can only imagine what Gatsby-esque scenes unfolded. There would be a boom – a warning shot across the bow of a gondola – and a sixty-tonne frigate would loom into view from behind the lake's island. The gardens would then be engulfed in a mock sea battle, the air thick with razzmatazz and gunpowder, superseded only by a display of shimmering fireworks which, resounding off the Chilterns, would light up the golden globe on top of the church spire – designed by Dashwood to seat six – like a glittering moon orbiting the park.

For those already smarting at Dashwood's hedonism, I'm afraid this is only the beginning. For as the fireworks fizzled out into the sky, and the landscape was plunged into darkness, Dashwood's guests would have already dissipated, shrieking and whooping, into the gardens. Whilst some may have gone to the Temple of the Winds to gamble away their fortunes at whist, or others rowed to the Island's Temple of Music to jive a cotillion, the more devious still would have made for the garden's most infamous folly: the Temple of Venus.

When I first heard about West Wycombe's Temple of Venus, I was incredulous. How could a folly be so crude? Yes, the gardens are more compact than those at Stourhead or Stowe, making the experience more intense. And yes, the follies are canary yellow, lending them a certain lurid *je ne sais quoi*. But that hardly constitutes an 18+ folly.

Stomping through the garden after a particularly fraught drive, I was determined to remain unfazed. Nevertheless, on turning the corner, what I saw was enough to make even the most seasoned voyeur blush: a mound, perforated by a hole, from which spread two wings topped with a tempietto. It was, in other words, the architectural representation of a vagina.

The more I stared at the folly – or rather, glanced – the more it seemed to me that it was the lynchpin to the garden. Its elegant tempietto and statues symbolised the house, with its many columns and objets d'art on the hill above, the mound represented the gardens, whilst the flinty opening below suggested the most secretive and spectacular aspect of West Wycombe: its caves, Dashwood's private Hades, and the Hellfire Club that frequented them.

It is for good reason that Francis Dashwood was described by a now frankly intimidated Walpole as having 'the staying power of a stallion and the impetuosity of a bull'. In order to exercise this, he founded yet another club: The Knights of St Francis of Wycombe – another swipe at the Catholic continent. Membership for this was drawn from all of Dashwood's other clubs and included the First Lord of the Admiralty, the Archbishop of Canterbury's son, poets, painters and dons, as well as occasional visitors such as Benjamin Franklin or, amazingly, a dissolute

The Temple of Venus | 79

young John Wesley. The motto of the club was '*Fais Ce Que Tu Voudras*' ('Do as You Wish'), and though its activities were mainly focused on ritualistic sex parties at Medmenham Abbey, they also met in the caves of West Wycombe.

After buying a ticket from a guide whose cheerfulness was utterly incongruous with the Gothic setting, I headed down into the caves. I had mixed feelings about this. On the one hand, it was exciting. These caves were, after all, one of the most impressive underground complexes in England, thought to be designed after the Eleusinian Mysteries of Ancient Greece. On the other hand, my determination to remain unfazed was faltering. As with any self-respecting cave, they have acquired a number of Gothic tales. Some talk of 'The White Lady', a socially aspirational servant who met a sticky end, others of courtesans, dressed as hooded nuns, disappearing into the gloom below, or, perhaps most famously, the club's steward, Paul Whitehead, searching for his heart.

Whilst I didn't encounter a forlorn Whitehead, the reality was surreal enough without him. A series of swoops, swerves, twists and turns led me deep into the ground. One moment I was passing a number of chambers cut into the rock, another I was in a cavernous oval chamber, where I imagined the aforementioned bacchanalia might have continued, before heading still further down into the lair reserved for Dashwood's most depraved friends. The air was now musty and cold, it was five minutes until closing, and I felt increasingly uncomfortable.

Stumbling to the end of the passage, I found myself on a bridge which crossed over an underground river, once only possibly by boat, on the other side of which lay the final chamber: the Inner Temple. Peering through the grille, I imagined Dashwood's 'sides shaking with laughter and ... nostrils with snuff', to quote one contemporary, or the moment the Club released a baboon dressed as the Devil on Lord Sandwich. This caused the latter to cry 'spare a wretch who was

80 | *Follies*

never sincerely your servant. I sinned only from the vanity of being in the fashion.' Indeed, The Inner Temple is a place where several fashions converge: the Age of Sentiment, the Exotic, the Gothic and the sublime, bubbling over into an orgiastic fantasy, summarised by an inscription on the spire three hundred feet above: 'Memento'. Whether this means '*Memento Mori*' ('Remember You Must Die'), or '*Memento Meri*' ('Remember to Drink the Wine'), we do not know. Either way, I turned on my heel and ran.

Just when you think you've got to the bottom of Francis Dashwood, he surprises you. Despite his debauchery, he not only reformed the postal service into something of a national enterprise but revised the Prayer Book and tried to avoid confrontation with America. Even the caves, a symbol of his depravity, were designed to relieve local unemployment using a scheme he proposed during a brief stint as Chancellor of the Exchequer. He was, in other words, a libertarian as much as he was a libertine. To quote his *Address to the Gentlemen, Clergy and Freeholders of … Great Britain*:

> Man – has a natural Right to be free. By Freedom is not nor can be meant, that every Individual should act as he lists, and according as he is swayed by his own Passion, Vices or Infirmities: but Freedom is a Right every Man has to do what he will with his own, conformable to Law; is a Right every Man has to be judged impartially by his Equals and to have his Property secured to him as his Posterity.

With the Dashwoods continuing to live at West Wycombe today, there may be something in this.

Clytha Castle | 81

As now demonstrated at West Wycombe, Stourhead and Kew, the second half of the eighteenth century was a cauldron of contrasting styles and influences. Whilst the Whigs championed the idea of a Saxon England, artistic circles became increasingly preoccupied with the power of emotion over thought. These trends were fuelled by the steady influx of ideologies from the East, as well as the ongoing discovery of ancient ones in the ashes of Herculaneum and Pompeii. The tectonic plates of culture were shifting once more. By the mid eighteenth century, this resulted not in the permutation of an old style but the formation of an entirely new one: the Gothick. This was a molten fusion of classical proportion and Gothic detailing that proclaimed an older, freer England, whilst simultaneously hinting at other, decidedly more multicultural undercurrents. Its maestro was none other than Horace Walpole.

As an experimental style, the Gothick was not initially trusted for proper building, so its champions turned to the best alternative for its development: the folly, through which it simmered in parallel with the Palladian, neoclassical and exotic. Although Walpole's villa at Strawberry Hill is generally considered the best example of the Gothick, I am not convinced. To quote a frazzled Walpole: 'My whole time is passed in giving tickets for seeing it, and hiding myself when it is seen – take my advice, never build a charming house for yourself between London and Hampton Court, everybody will live in it but you.'

Taking his advice, I set my satnav for a far wilder part of England: Monmouthshire, the nether zone between England and Wales, once ruled by the March Lords, which was not formally merged with Wales until 1972. Appropriately, in this ancient frontier, studded with real ruins and castles, we find one of the best examples of Walpole's new 'Gothick frontier': Clytha Castle, a fabulous fairy-tale structure, otherwise known as the 'Taj Mahal of Wales'.

82 | *Follies*

As I skirted south of the Shropshire Mynds, deciduous woodland was replaced with swathes of fir, the hills became more angular and the skies a marbled blue. Not long after crossing the River Severn, I saw a rupture in the ground flash past me. This was Offa's Dyke – the Hadrian's Wall of Wales – and I knew I had passed from Mercia into the Kingdom of Gwent. As I wound my way deeper into the country, the signs became increasingly complex. Guttural names like 'The Narth', 'Govilon', and 'Llangattock-Vibon-Avel' came and went, speaking of the Celts who sailed up the Severn from Northern Spain, the giant Clytha for whom this was his 'stomping ground', of Welsh princes and mountain gold.

After passing the Clytha Arms, I found myself driving down a hill between two steep banks of rock. This was followed by an archway of trees which opened onto the Usk Valley: a sweeping view ending in the Skirrid, Sugar Loaf and Black Mountains beyond. Finally, on the opposite hill, guarding the entrance to the valley, was Clytha Castle.

At first sight from the car, with its towers and crenellations, Clytha looks like a perfectly normal castle. Look again, however, and you risk veering off the road. For linking the towers is one of the oddest architectural features I have ever seen: a crenellated 'curtain wall' that swoops down from a sort of coronet, linking the building together, like two lopsided smiles fringed with jagged teeth. Despite its surreal appearance, the wall works surprisingly well – with a faint whiff of the Alhambra about it. Beyond this are all the usual features: pointed windows, fitted with intricate sashes, a string course of trefoils, quatrefoils and an apricot plaster render which, in both colour and meteorological optimism, lifts the building clean out of the imagination.

It's fair to say the Gothick owes more to literature than any other architectural style. It is no coincidence that it took off shortly after Horace Walpole published *The Castle of Otranto* in 1764, nor that he referred to Strawberry Hill as 'my little Otranto'. Though a hilariously bad novel, with its ancient legends, presumptuous hermits, accidental infanticides and death by giant helmet – possibly the greatest non-sequitur in literature – it is considered by many to be the first in the Gothic canon. Nevertheless, despite its literary genesis, Gothick architecture is not meant to be read literally. If it is, you soon realise that it is a papier-mâché hodgepodge of medieval detail thrown together merely to satisfy Walpole and his 'Committee of Taste' – i.e. his friends. Instead, as seen in Stourhead's King Alfred's Tower, the Gothick is guided by associationism. Through a bizarre combination of elements bordering on the uncanny, it is designed not to 'tell' but to 'trigger' a series of images: a process that relies as much on the viewer's imagination as it does the architect's skill. Looking back to Clytha, my imagination was rioting. In other words, it was not impossible to believe that behind Clytha's mysterious curtain wall lay the towers, galleries, dungeons and vaults of Otranto.

Walpole aside, as you get closer to the building, you realise that it is also Gothic in its own right. For in the middle is a plaque that explains it was built in 1790 by William Jones: 'for the purpose of relieving a mind sincerely afflicted by the loss of the most excellent Wife' – hence the Taj comparison. However, much as we might like to try and compare the unlikely Welsh squire to Shah Jahan, this story could not be more Gothic if it tried. Clytha conjures up images of a man, wild with grief, trying to tame his passions through stone – a precursor to the tortuous poetry of the romantics. The story is not dissimilar to the genesis of the most famous Gothick building of all, the now collapsed Fonthill Abbey, whose designer – William Beckford – once said: 'Some people drink to forget their unhappiness. I do not drink, I build. And it ruins me.'

Taking one last look at Clytha, it seemed to me that, stylistically, I had gone full circle. Whilst the buildings at the beginning of this book were essentially Gothic, with increasing levels of classical detail, this

84 | *Follies*

was a classical frame, with high levels of Gothic detailing. Though we might smirk at both Walpole and his Gothick, they symbolise an age-old tug of war over the identity of an island nation, and one that

is particularly relevant today: are we English or are we European? Do we use the Gothic, symbolic of England's sovereignty, or the classical, representing the philosophy and reason of Ancient Greece? Though we

86 | *Follies*

have seen this before in Smythson's French-cum-castle Prodigy Houses, Vanbrugh's English Baroque, and the muscular Palladianism of Kent and Wood, it is in the Gothick that the debate perhaps reaches a final, more imaginative attempt at a compromise. In its own funny way then, Clytha is a castle: a place that attempts to keep the peace – and does so with an architectural sense of humour.

Whilst Clytha Castle may be associated with appeasement, my next site, Broadway Tower, situated on the border between Gloucestershire and Worcestershire, is a proper castle, associated with national defence. Even before it was built, its site, the second-highest point in the Cotswolds, was well known as 'Beacon Hill', used for signalling everything from invasion of the Welsh to the distant sails of the Spanish Armada. By the late eighteenth century, its spectacular setting and story were crying out for a folly. After dropping a couple of hints, the distinguished Capability Brown, now author of almost two hundred gardens, persuaded the Earl of Coventry to commission one. Coventry didn't dare contradict the 'father of modern gardening', and the up and coming architect, James Wyatt, designer of Fonthill Abbey, was engaged to build a 'Saxon Tower'. And so it was that one of England's most iconic buildings was born.

Given the eighteenth century's fantastically lax definition of 'Saxon', I was curious to see what Coventry and Wyatt had come up with. A belvedere perhaps – with all the swoops and swirls of the Gothick? Or maybe another King Alfred's Tower – standing tall and gaunt against the skyline?

Crossing over the brow of the hill, what I saw was far more impressive: a giant rook. The ground swells to a natural peak where three cylindrical turrets contain a hexagonal keep which rises from a wide

base to a series of Romanesque windows. These open onto six balconies, decorated with intersecting arcades, echoing the battlements above from which, on a clear day, you can see sixteen counties and the spire of Worcester Cathedral. The overall composition is stupendous. Despite its miniature size, French windows and balconies, the building exudes

88 | *Follies*

all the confidence and weight of a Norman stronghold. It is as though an entire citadel jostles between its towers, as though every castle learnt about in childhood, Caernarfon, Dover, Warwick and Leeds, wait to rear up from behind the next turret. If a symbol of national security could be transformed into a building, then this is it.

On its completion, sources disagree as to the use of the Tower. Some claim that it was a signalling station to warn staff when the Coventries were nearing home. Others claim that the Countess, Barbara, used it to 'study the stars' with her handsome young astrologer. Whatever the truth, its later use is by far the most interesting – and in keeping with its design. In the early nineteenth century, it was turned into a press by Sir Thomas Phillipps, who owned sixty thousand manuscripts ranging from medieval charters to French romances, poems, letters and deeds. As one friend wrote: 'Broadway Tower is like a lighthouse, signalling to the friends of letters that a hospitable roof exists, under which all pilgrims of learning are made welcome.' This, however, was only the beginning. In 1866, Cormell Price, the 'Knight of Broadway Tower', took over the tower as a country retreat. Price was a second-wave pre-Raphaelite who believed that the art should return to an earlier medieval style that predated Raphael. At Broadway, he hosted a steady stream of fellow pre-Raphaelites, from artists Edward Burne-Jones and Dante Gabriel Rossetti to William Morris, the designer, craftsman, socialist and poet, titan of the nineteenth century and father of the Arts and Crafts movement.

Finally, Broadway Tower came into its own. During visits, Morris and his family would visit local villages and churches during the day, or picnic on the close-cropped rolling hills before returning to the Tower. Here, they would bathe on the roof, allowing the 'clean aromatic wind to blow the aches out of our tired bodies' – whilst trying to stop the soap being blown away at the same time. In the evening, in what Morris described as the 'Tower among the winds and the clouds', I imagine the assembled company chatting late into the night; the light of the fire flickering across their gigantic beards as they discuss Arthurian legends, craftsmanship and the writings of John Ruskin, thus enacting their holy mantra: 'Fellowship is life, and lack of fellowship is death.'

Nevertheless, the tower was not purely whimsical. So inspiring was its atmosphere that on one visit Morris was moved to start the Society for the Protection of Ancient Buildings. It also served as a hub for the Cotswolds Arts and Crafts movement, whose echoes can still be felt in places like Chipping Campden today. The Tower was, in essence, both a rural retreat and an intellectual stronghold. It was a place where the pseudo-Gothic ideas carved onto its façade by Wyatt a century before reached fruition in the minds and actions of its weekenders, who regarded themselves as knights on a quest to save England. Their dragon, however, was not the absence of Christianity, which preoccupied the generation before, but imperial capitalism, which they wished to replace with an older world of hand-made goods, local government and rural living. As Morris wrote:

> art will make our streets as beautiful as the woods, as elevating as the mountain-sides: it will be a pleasure and a rest, and not a weight upon the spirits to come from the open country into a town; every man's house will be fair and decent, soothing to his mind and helpful to his work … every man will have his share of the BEST … It is a dream, you may say, of what has never been and never will be; true, it has never been, and therefore, since the world is alive, and moving yet, my hope is the greater that it one day will be.

At Broadway Tower, that dream seemed within reach. This, however, was not the end of the Tower's story. Like the chess piece which it resembles, it came sweeping back into the picture in WWII as a station for the Royal Observer Corps – the twentieth-century equivalent of

90 | *Follies*

the Elizabethan beacon, known by the codename 'Russian Orthodox Church' – to warn the nearby cities of the Luftwaffe, whilst during the Cold War, the premises was used as a nuclear bunker from which to monitor the distant explosions of enemy bombs. Inspecting the bunker, I half expected to see James Bond zip wire in from the roof. In the event of a real Armageddon, its operators were provided not with gadgets but several feet of concrete, Monopoly, Cluedo and a strict no-dog policy.

As I left the Tower, it comforted me to think that whatever the world throws at us next, be it dragons, bombs or pandemics, Broadway Tower will still stand, watching over the west of England: Stratford-upon-Avon, the Battle of Edgehill, Tewkesbury Abbey, the Vale of the Red Horse, Cleeve Cloud, the Malvern Hills, Wychwood Forest, Woodstock and, as the sign put it, the 'Industrial City of Birmingham'. A milky silhouette against a crystalline sky, it is the 007 of follies: cold and aloof from a distance but with a certain twinkle up close. Thank God it's only armed with board games.

From Broadway, we move from a building worthy of Bond to a palace fit for his nemeses. I came across this by pure chance. Owing to a puncture, I had to call a taxi to take me to where I was staying the night. In the pocket of the car door, however, I found a brochure for perhaps the most extraordinary-looking building I had ever seen: a Mughal country house. This wasn't far away at all, so I quickly rang the owner, who kindly agreed to see me, and the taxi was duly diverted to Sezincote House.

Though 'Sezincote' may sound exotic, it is in fact an English name that dates back to Doomsday. Whilst '*la chene*' means oak in French, 'cot' is the Old English for shelter or dwelling, and so the two words combine to create: 'Home of the Oaks'. Passing along the estate's cottages and crumbly drystone walls, there was little to suggest otherwise. As we swept through the house's verdant park, I even began to wonder whether I had the wrong address. Suddenly I saw the glint of a green copper dome above the trees, and my doubts were dispelled.

As we pulled up outside the house, I looked at the taxi driver and we both beamed in disbelief. Standing before us was what can only be described as the Taj Mahal in Gloucestershire – a folly by force of its sheer eccentricity. In the place of the Taj's giant arch is a central bay in amber stone. This is bordered by a series of windows interlaced with blind ogee arches and octagonal turrets. The windows, carved in the shape of peacock tails, fan into lotus flowers which, in turn, rise to a *chaija* – or heavily projecting cornice. This swells into a mint-green Saracenic dome, copied from Lal Bagh Gate at Faizabad, flanked by intricate *chhatri*. We were gobsmacked: whoever built this place had clearly been to India – and not just for a holiday.

This, however, is only the start. An orangery unfurls away from the house and into a pavilion. This is decorated with fifteen French windows, again peacock in design, from which the smell of white ginger lily, passionflower and jasmine drifted across the lawn and into the gardens. Immediately before the house is the 'Paradise Garden', copying the manmade 'Elysium' that surrounds many of India's mausoleums, first designed by Mughal Emperor Babur. In the centre is an octagonal fountain, representing the squaring of a circle and the reconciliation of man's life with eternity. From here emanate two canals flanked by clipped evergreens which, again, divide the garden into four sections interspersed with lines of Persian poetry, representing the rivers of life and the meeting between the temporal and the eternal.

The spiritual theme continues deeper into the garden. Again, it is centred around water. At the top of a stream is the Temple of Surya,

the Hindu god of the sun, illuminated every day by the first stroke of morning light. Before it spreads a pool whose clay bed lends the water a silver quality, reflected in the trees and plants around it. The water trickles down to a bridge whose foundations form a series of stepping stones – similar to a scheme designed by Emperor Jahangir at Shalimar Bagh – where you can sit and admire the view whilst the water rushes under your feet. Look up and you see the statue of Surya. Look down and you see the Serpent Pool where water spurts out of the fangs of a three-headed snake – another symbol of regeneration – before descending to the lake at the bottom of the hill and the English park beyond. Wandering back up through the garden, its leaves bursting with colour from the silver shimmer of a weeping pear to the jewel-like pendulums of a bleeding heart, crimson flash of Persian ironwood and thicket of green bamboo, I had only one thought: who was the English Kubla Khan behind this idyllic place?

Back at the house, I was quickly filled in by its tall and genial owner, Edward Peake. After being led through an exquisite neoclassical interior – which seemed to belong to an entirely different house – of canary-yellow silks, murals and a staircase that flings itself across the hall, I found myself in a jumble of back passages. Here, surrounded by a ping-pong table, water guns, hockey sticks and music practice – as well as a defunct bowler hat – Edward made me a cup of tea and told all.

In 1795, John Cockerell, great-great nephew of the diarist Samuel Pepys, returned from India where he had been working for the East India Company with his half Indian wife, Estuarta, and their children, and bought Sezincote. On his death in 1798, his final wish was not to have all traces of the source of his wealth hidden – as with most outgoing merchants – but instead proclaimed in the transformation of Sezincote into an Indian house. This task fell to Charles, John's younger brother, who asked Samuel Pepys Cockerell, another brother, to come up with the design. S.P. Cockerell was a talented architect who pulled the artist Thomas Daniell onto the job. This was a clever move because Daniell had just returned from India where he had sketched a huge number of temples, mosques, tombs, houses, palaces and their gardens, published in his book *Oriental Scenery*. He was, in essence, one of the few people in Europe who understood how Indian architecture worked.

The combined talent of Daniell and Cockerell meant that Sezincote benefitted from the best of both worlds: one famed for its palaces and tombs, the other for its country houses; one speaking of great cosmopolitan capitals, processions of elephants and Samarkand, the other the opening lines of Henry James' *The Portrait of a Lady*. When you combine the house with the gardens, thought to have been designed by Brown's heir, Humphry Repton, the result is spellbinding.

Unlike Brighton Pavilion – the closest thing to it in England – Sezincote has an impressive stylistic integrity. Whilst Brighton is a potpourri of oriental-cum-exotic forms that borders on satire, Sezincote, though also an architectural blend, is undeniably Indian – or rather, Mughal. Perhaps the reason it works so well is because Mughal architecture itself is a style of compromise – not unlike Clytha's Gothick. In the second half of the sixteenth century, Emperor Akbar championed a new style that incorporated both Hindu and Muslim detailing in order to placate the different religions of the now vast Mughal empire, resulting in the Taj Mahal a century later. In the same way, Sezincote respectfully combines *chija, chhatris* and a dome with sash windows, a Greek interior and classical proportions to form a unique style of unabashed Anglo-Indian architecture that recognises the merits of both styles. It is the only example like it in Northern Europe.

There is, however, another reason that Sezincote is so rare. At the same time that it was being built, the nature of the imperial project was becoming more sinister. Replacing a culture of – albeit ruthless

96 | *Follies*

– mercantile co-habitation, where figures such as Cockerell adopted local clothes and intermarried, came one of strict segregation based on a sense of cultural, and especially religious, superiority. Though the British had appropriated a host of other styles, and thus their value systems as well, they would not do so with Indian architecture because of its perceived inferiority. It is for this reason that when Sezincote was sold in 1880, the description of the house studiously avoided its unusual style. Sezincote, in other words, became a rebel house, an illustration of the fatuousness of the imperial notion of cultural superiority – an excuse for economic exploitation – and was thus quietly brushed under the carpet.

Fortunately, Sezincote is back to its usual self today. In the downstairs loo, military photographs and pictures of sports teams are replaced by Edward's certificates in Persian, as well as photographs of fantastic Mughal parties and weddings – for which the house is a frequent venue. Just as I thought the place couldn't get any more magical, Edward turned to me and said: 'Oh, before I forget, would you like to see a new Betjeman poem about the house – it's just been discovered. He used to stay here with Clement Attlee as a student.' Of course I bloody did – and how apt it was:

If those domes could only speak,
If those turnip tops could talk,
If those wonderfully life-like Nandi bulls
Could rise on their legs and walk;

If those prickles and spikes and carvings
Could climb from each golden wall
And march in a phalanx of stone and lead
Into the entrance hall;

What would they say to the Colonel
As they crowded the graceful stairs
And overflowed in the ballroom
And sat on the Empire chairs?

… 'When the starlight shone on the stonework
Out of the Cotswold sky,
They admired that crescent of Indian art
As the English clouds went by.

In the same way that the name 'Sezincote', Home of the Oaks, is formed of two wildly different cultures, French and Saxon, so too is the house. A dazzling example not so much of cultural appropriation but cultural approbation, conveyed, once again, through the folly.

To me, at least, the Victorians were not great folly builders and will thus be summarily leapfrogged. This is not because they did not build – far from it – but rather because the evangelising-cum-imperial crusade that so often guided their design process was antithetical to the spirit of follies. For the Victorians, everything had to be first, a tower. Second, a very big tower. Third, a tower with a job. Thus, castles such as Clytha and Broadway evolved into stupendous sizes and were assigned new functions: from giant clocks to memorials and water towers – all, I might add, with a decidedly phallic touch. Instead, whimsy was invested not in the landscape but in the buildings themselves: Big Ben, the Natural History Museum, Royal Courts of Justice and St Pancras Hotel. These were built in a variety of 'neo' styles from the neo-Gothic, under the aegis of Augustus Pugin and George

98 | *Follies*

Gilbert Scott, to the neo-Jacobethan under Charles Barry, connected by a series of increasingly ambitious stations and bridges made possible by a new figure on the architectural scene, 'the engineer'. This was best summed up by Isambard Kingdom Brunel – a name so bombastic you can practically hear the dynamite – author of the Forth Road Bridge or Paddington Station, whose black chimney-pipe top hat, chops and steady, unfazed expression came to define the age. Arguably, it was these new buildings that replaced the folly; constructions at once so specific and yet nonsensical that, beyond schools and psychiatric hospitals, or both, we are still struggling to find uses for them today.

This, however, was not the end of follies. Instead, like a resistance movement, they went into hiding for almost a century. First, with the pre-Raphaelites, then the Arts and Crafts movement, the Decadent movement, the Art Nouveau and Deco. Finally, with the blaring of jazz after WWI, whimsy was back on the menu. In 1935, the folly made a spectacular return thanks to one of the period's most celebrated hosts. This was Lord Berners, a talented composer, whose visitor's book sounds like an extract from *Midnight in Paris*, featuring the likes of Salvador Dali, Igor Stravinsky, Nancy Mitford, Edith Sitwell, H.G. Wells, Gertrude Stein, John Betjeman and Diana Mosley.

Even in a period famous for its non-conformity, Berners was a legendary eccentric. As a child, on hearing that dogs could be taught to swim by being thrown into water, he attempted to teach his to fly by throwing it out of the window. Fortunately it survived, but he nearly didn't. This alternative take on life continued into adulthood where he was famous for keeping a flock of fantailed doves in colours of the rainbow, for storing a small clavichord to play in his Rolls-Royce and for often inviting a horse to tea.

In 1919, Berners heard that the Scots pines on top of a much-loved local hill at Faringdon were going to be felled. In order to save them, he

Faringdon Tower | 99

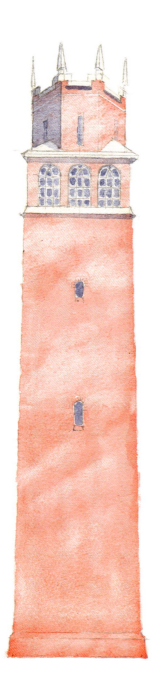

bought the land. One day, he was walking there and commented that 'this hill needs a tower' – a comment that attracted such consternation that its realisation became irresistible. Here, Berners encountered the new nemesis of the folly: the planning committee. When they inquired as to the point of Faringdon Tower, Berners duly informed them that it had none. Eventually Berners won, but conceded on health and safety by including a plaque that read: 'Members of the Public committing suicide from this Tower do so at their own risk.' Finally, the tower was built and given to Berners' lover, Robert Heber-Percy, as a twenty-fourth birthday present – the latter commenting that he would have preferred a pony.

After scrambling my way up a sandy bank and into the wood, I found myself agreeing that the hill did indeed benefit from the tower. It was, however, a very odd and faintly familiar design: a pillar of brick rising to a viewing room, topped with a jagged cluster of obelisks. This, it transpired, is the result of yet another spat. Berners had commissioned his friend, Lord Wellesley, to build the tower – a joke as the style was to be Gothic, which Wellesley resolutely loathed. Whilst

100 | *Follies*

Berners was away on holiday, Wellesley got his own back by building the tower in a classical design which, when Berners finally saw it, was reversed at the eleventh hour, hence its mongrel scheme.

I turned to leave. As I did so, however, the sun went behind the clouds and the tower turned from a bright red to a dusty blue, utterly transforming its appearance. Suddenly, I knew what it reminded me of: Sauron's Tower, or Isengard, to the Tolkienian aficionado, surrounded by a ring of Ents. As Tolkien wrote:

> There stood a tower of marvellous shape. It was fashioned by the builders of old, who smoothed the Ring of Isengard, and yet it seemed a thing not made by the craft of Men ... near the summit they opened into gaping horns, their pinnacles sharp as the points of spears, keen-edged as knives. Between them was a narrow space, and there upon a floor of polished stone, written with strange signs, a man might stand five hundred feet above the plain.

After a quick google, it turned out that this was no coincidence. According to recent research by John Garth, Tolkien – who used to compare the mystery of bygone poetry to an ancient tower in his lectures down the road in Oxford – did indeed use Faringdon as his inspiration.

Beyond design, the towers have more in common. Just as darkness looms in *The Lord of the Rings*, so too did it for Faringdon in the outbreak of WWII, only four years after its completion. As with many follies, it was manned by the 1940s' answer to Hobbits, the Home Guard, who used it as a viewing platform.

Today, Faringdon is a much-used local site which proudly proclaims that it has 'no facilities whatsoever'. In 2000, it was fitted with a beacon of light, rendering it one of the only – if not *the* only – landlocked lighthouses in England.

As I drove away, the tower beaming in the distance, there was something powerful about it: as though the folly, admittedly ridiculous in premise, stands to represent the glimmer of peace that existed between the wars – be they of men, wizards, or perhaps a bit of both.

As modern styles of painting, poetry, prose, music and fashion were being forged in Lord Berner's drawing room, so too were they evolving in architecture. Just like classicism four hundred years before, this new style had its roots in the continent, developed by names such as Mies van der Rohe, Walter Gropius and Le Corbusier. In time-honoured fashion, these designers, with their bow ties and clinical, thick-rimmed spectacles, sought a clean break from older styles, replacing them with one that adequately reflected the age of science, mechanisation and democracy. This time they meant it. In order to achieve this, they turned design philosophy inside out, with emphasis no longer on fussy detail but rather on form and the ideas that it could convey. This was invariably expressed in the new wonder kid of materials: reinforced concrete.

In England – ever slow to latch on – nowhere is this better illustrated than in the post-war New Towns, a utopian project designed to make modern living conditions freely available to all. In spite of their low budgets, these projects were often finished with a piece of art in order to add a local landmark. Quite why they felt that fake hippos, giant flowers or even concrete cows – as seen in Milton Keynes – were appropriate, I will never fathom. This was taken most seriously at Peterlee in County Durham, a new town for miners whose artistic design was presided over by Victor Pasmore, the legendary abstract artist. Rather than a statue, Pasmore believed that the town needed something more

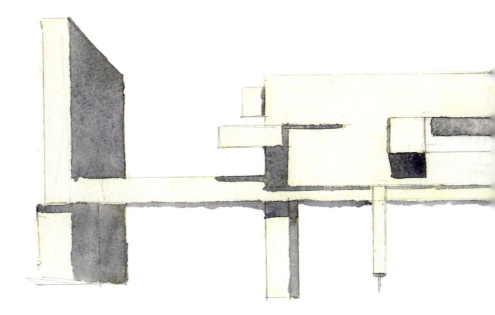

substantial. As such, he came up with the idea of an empty modernist pavilion to act as an iconic focal point for the housing estate in much the same way that Kent used follies for the rural equivalent. Thus a modernist folly was born. Pasmore even went as far as to call it 'The Apollo Pavilion' – not to a god but, in the spirit of 1969, something far better: the first man on the moon.

Driving through Peterlee, I couldn't miss the pavilion. Situated in the centre of a public park, it may as well have come from outer space. A shallow lawn rolls down to a serpentine lake over which floats what, at a glance, looks like an unfinished game of Jenga: a series of interlinked cream cubes centred around a sort of pillbox that cast a series of crisp, angular shadows, reflected in the water below. Compared to endless columns, crenellations and domes, this sight came as a refreshing change. Here, I use refreshing in the ice-cold plunge pool sense. For some, it's a

masochistic heaven: as though a needle has pricked every pore of your body, sending an electric thrill up the spine akin to downing a pint of Tabasco. For others, its epicurean hell: an annual torture that makes the mind go numb, endured solely for the sake of posturing. When it comes to modern architecture, the former stance tends to belong to those who see the ideas behind the buildings, whilst the latter belongs to the more literal viewer, who see simply what stands before them.

Personally, however dull, brutal and graffiti ridden this type of architecture may seem, it cannot be divorced from the ideas that underpin it – and as ideas go, they're pretty inspiring. To quote Pasmore:

> If we take a sheet of paper and scribble on it vigorously we become involved in the process of bringing into being something concrete and visible which was not there before … The more we concentrate

104 | *Follies*

on this operation, the more we are drawn into it both emotionally and intellectually. But as the line develops organically, in accordance with the process of scribbling, we find ourselves directing its course towards a particular but unknown end; until finally an image appears which surprises us by its familiarity and touches us as if awakening forgotten memories buried long ago. We have witnessed not only an evolution, but also a metamorphosis.

Through the Apollo Pavilion, Pasmore hoped to achieve the same metamorphosis socially; that in providing a 'free anonymous environment … through which to walk, in which to linger and on which to play', the Pavilion would 'because of its independence … lift the activity and psychology of an urban housing community on to a universal plane'.

But within ten years, the Pavilion had turned grey, been covered with graffiti and had become a hub for all the usual activities. By the 1980s, residents even began to call for its removal. Nevertheless, in 1998, English Heritage attempted to list the building, and everything changed. Though this failed initially, it resulted in a steering group that culminated in the Pavilion's restoration in 2009 and eventual listing in 2011. Soon after followed an incredible series of events: a brass band from Rajasthan, fifteen-piece jazz band from Milan and performance of *Twelfth Night*. Complimenting this was an outreach programme for local schoolchildren whose activities ranged from a dance summer school to photography seminars and poetry workshops. Last year, the Pavilion's fiftieth birthday celebrations included a giant inflatable sculpture, film screenings and exhibition, all recorded in the national press.

Though the Pavilion's aesthetic merit remains a moot point, and the success of the New Towns in which it was conceived remain highly debatable, its status as an emblem of hope and regeneration, as well as the use of a folly today, is in no doubt. Pasmore's vision of social metamorphosis through abstract architecture might have stumbled, but it triumphed in the long run. As a resident wrote in one of the poetry workshops, the Pavilion is:

A synthesis of art
And architecture
Apollo optimism
Geometric planes in white
Span a vision
Of pure imagination

In the early hours of 6 August 1986, the residents of New High Street, Headington, woke to see one of the most surreal sights in Europe: a fully sized shark, gills and all, face-planted into the roof of a two-storey terraced house, as though it had just plummeted from the skies.

Despite its fame, nothing can prepare you for the Headington Shark. On first sight, it reminded me of an extract from Douglas Adams' equally surreal *The Hitchhiker's Guide to the Galaxy*, where an intergalactic missile is accidentally transformed into a sperm whale and fired at the earth. In what must be, in my humble opinion, one of funniest monologues of all time, Douglas records the whale's first, and indeed last, thoughts. These range from: 'Er, excuse me, who am I? Hello? Why am I here? What's my purpose in life? What do I mean by who am I?' to the touching ending:

What's this thing suddenly coming towards me very fast? Very very fast. So big and flat and round, it needs a big wide sounding name

106 | *Follies*

like… ow… ound… round… ground! That's it! That's a good name
– ground! I wonder if it will be friends with me?

Though this extract may seem almost as much of a non-sequitur as the
Shark, it is the closest I can get to describing the sensation of seeing it.
Not only do both share a total sense of incongruity but an uncomfortable sense of existentialism, as well as a macabre, somewhat unnerving
sense of humour. The Shark is, in other words, a postmodern folly.

Like the Apollo Pavilion, this folly also had a political motivation.
It was cooked up over a glass of wine on the doorstep between the
journalist Bill Heine – from whose house it eventually protruded – and
sculptor John Buckley. Heine was furious about the American bombing
of Libya, whose planes could be seen taking off from Heyford outside
Oxford, and wanted to erect a monument in protest, as well as to record
the anniversary of the dropping of the atomic bomb on Nagasaki. In
order to hit home, the pair wanted something that conveyed the utter
helplessness of those experiencing raids. Sharks, which attack their prey
by hurtling out of the deep, provided an apt metaphor. After being
designed over a couple of months, built from fibreglass and dropped
into the roof by crane overnight, the pair celebrated its completion with
champagne on the roof and eagerly awaited its reception.

Needless to say, Oxford City Council didn't get it. Nevertheless,
there is no law forbidding the erection of fibreglass sharks on private
property, and so they struggled to get rid of it. First, they tried to
argue that the Shark was a danger to the public. After inspecting the
girders specially designed to support it, however, this transpired to be
false. Then they tried to cart it off to a museum. In a final bureau-
cratic masterstroke, they refused an application for 'Retention of public
sculpture', and so Heine appealed to the then Secretary of State for the
Environment, Michael Heseltine. Heseltine's finding is an entertaining

108 | *Follies*

read and possibly the best justification for folly building that I have ever read – one that echoes Erasmus's *In Parise of Folly*:

> The contrast between the object and its setting is quite deliberate. In this sense, the work is specific to its setting, and it would 'read' quite differently in the context of, say, the foyer to an arts centre in Gloucester Green. It is (as the Council say) incongruous … It is the very same feature which appeals to many of the Shark's supporters, and which has made it an urban landmark… An 'incongruous' object can become accepted as a landmark in some cases becoming well-known, even well-loved, in the process. Something of this sort seems to have happened, for many people, to the Shark. There is a real sense in which permitting the Shark to remain is the "risky" option, the safe and easy thing to do being to remove it. However, I cannot believe that the purpose of planning control is to enforce a boring and mediocre uniformity to the built environment. Any system of control must make some small space for the dynamic, the unexpected and the downright quirky or we shall all be the poorer for it. I believe that this is one case where a little vision and imagination is appropriate, and I recommend that the Headington Shark be allowed to remain.

As a result, the Shark still waggles its tail out of 2 New High Street today. Its fibreglass body is not only a defiant symbol of peace, as relevant today as it was when it first crashed through the roof, but also an enduring landmark representing the rights of free speech, private property and artistic expression over state power. As the saying goes: a man's home is his castle – or, in this case, his aquarium.

The Teapot Obelisk | 109

Since the Shark, there has been something of a renaissance in traditional folly building. There could be many reasons for this. Perhaps it is because we live in an age of individualism? Or because the restrained classical aesthetic chimes with our own? Or perhaps because we seek escapism from a world where technology, for all its glory, leaves little room for mystery and rarely affords us a break? Whatever the reason, it's good news.

In the 1970s, Lord McAlpine had an obelisk constructed with the words: 'This monument was built with a great deal of money which otherwise some day would have been given into the hands of public revenue.' Whilst more recently, Isabel and Julian Bannerman have promoted the use of more organic materials, constructing Inigo Jones-esque temples from wood with antlers in the frieze. This style has been championed by HRH the Prince of Wales in his country house at Highgrove.

At the time of writing, the latest folly to be completed was for Nicholas Coleridge, Chairman of the Victoria and Albert Museum, at his home in Worcestershire. After a powerful Bloody Mary, he showed me the building. Designed by Quinlan Terry, it is a curious octagonal structure in cut brick. On the outside, it seems half Tudor, half Gothick, with buttresses, ogee windows and a bell-shaped turret, whilst the inside consists of a dining room below, and study above, complete with a gas fire, armchairs and Indian miniatures. Despite its recent completion, it looks, at a glance, as though the remains of a previous house. Seeing my confusion, Coleridge chuckled and said that this was the intended effect – to confuse art historians. On asking why he built it, he responded that he wanted somewhere to sunbathe nude. He then added, thoughtfully, that he wanted somewhere to get away from it all and to leave something behind for the county – though admitted he might need to chuck some yogurt on it to speed up the ageing process first.

My final folly, however, is located close to where my journey began. This is Deene Park in rural Northamptonshire, a place that spans the thousand or so years covered in this book, and has been home to the Brudenell family for over five hundred of them. Before the Norman Conquest, Deene belonged to Westminster Abbey. In 1514, it was leased to the Brudenells – who continued to pay the Church a rent of £18 a year until they bought the freehold in 1970. Throughout this time, the family lived fairly quietly, with a major event occurring roughly once a century or so. These ranged from marrying a daughter of the aforementioned recusant Sir Thomas Tresham to hotfooting it from the Parliamentarians, a son being kidnapped on a grand tour or an ancestor leading the Charge of the Light Brigade. The head and tail of his horse, Ronald, still stand in the house today. This developed organically, including elements from almost every period, from a grand hall to the usual line-up of classical rooms, whilst the estate includes formal gardens and a park.

As the millennium approached, something needed to be done to mark it. On the advice of Sir Tim Clifford, then Chairman of the National Galleries of Scotland, it was decided that an obelisk, an Egyptian funerary monument used to mark the passage of the sun, should be constructed at the end of the drive opposite the house. This, however, was no ordinary obelisk. At the top, in the place of the usual urn, is the stone effigy of a teapot. Why a teapot? Because its owner, the late Edmund Brudenell, who lovingly restored the house from a state of near dereliction, started every day with a cup of Earl Grey, and ended it with a cup of Lapsang Souchong – taken from a thermos in a small briefcase when travelling. It also serves as a memorial to his parents and those of his wife, Marian, as well as a marker for the Royal Air Force.

Staring at the obelisk, it seemed to capture the essence of follies. Not only was it built in a playful style, furnished with a good story

The Teapot Obelisk

and set in a beautiful landscape, but there was something else. The teapot is, of course, a symbol of the English: a stubborn and slightly peculiar bunch that insist on drinking the tepid dregs of a mildly exotic leaf – once again, imported from abroad – every afternoon, social call and crisis. Meanwhile, the obelisk is an otherworldly symbol of time. Cobble the two together, and the result is something that comes close to capturing the essence of follies. Ageing in the landscape, executed in a myriad of designs, they stand as a comforting reminder of the nation's sense of self, as well as how the important things in life never really change. The older the folly is, or at least appears to be, the more marked this comfort is – like a fabulous ottoman carpet, whose threads tighten with age and use. Near them, time curdles and you become aware of the many different people whose stories have been woven into this island. Indeed, take a step back, and perhaps the greatest folly of all is England itself.

Acknowledgements

For their kindness,
patience and critical eye:
Anthony Fraser
Antonia Weir
Esmé O'Keeffe
Euan Monaghan
Fiona Fraser
George Tomsett
Helena Irvine
Leonie Fraser
Lucia Medina Uriarte
Marina Fraser
Ralph Wade
Theo Shack
Tom Perrin

For their generosity:
Christopher Ridgway
Clovis and Lizzie Meath Baker
Edward Peake
Hilary Peters
New College, Oxford
Nick and Georgia Coleridge
Robert and Charlotte Brudenell
Rupert Nichol
Simon Dring
The Broadway Tower Volunteers
The Duke of Beaufort
The Landmark Trust

And for their inspiration:
Beatrice Groves
Jim Sheppe
John Eidinow
Kantik Ghosh
Melanie Collins
Peter Davidson
Richard Hudson
The Schützer-Weissmann Family

ZULEIKA
www.zuleika.london